GENITALIA: rhetoric and reticence in the early modern period

Clive Hart

$\mathcal{G}$

Gilliland Press

MMI

First published 2001 by

Gilliland Press
"Homeland"
2, The Street
Weeley
CLACTON-ON-SEA
Essex CO16 9JE
UK

email: kays@essex.ac.uk

website: www.gillilandpress.co.uk

ISBN 0-9537867-2-2

Printed in the United Kingdom by Gilliland Press

Some antient Philosophers have laboured to search out the naturall reason of this naturall shame, which the eyes conceive when the instruments of generation are set before them; and why the eares take offence to heare them named: and they marvell to see, that nature hath framed those parts with such diligence and carefulnesse, and for an end of such importance, as the immortalizing of mankind, and yet the wiser a man is, the more he groweth in dislike to behold or heare them spoken of. . . . and who so resteth not offended at those terms and actions of generation, giveth a sure token . . . that he is blockish.

—Juan Huarte, *The examination of mens wits* (1594) 264

CONTENTS

Preface

I have not attempted to add to the large body of literature exploring the history of early modern medical treatises dealing with sex, a small selection of which is listed in the bibliography. Other than in passing I am not concerned with errors and confusions about anatomical matters. My aim is rather to examine nuances of the language used by those writing both in Latin and in the vernacular when discussion of sexual matters becomes appropriate or necessary. As there are thousands of such treatises, my survey is necessarily selective. Anatomists constantly quoted, paraphrased, or expanded passages by their predecessors, making it often impossible to trace the true origin of a remark. Rather than embark on a hunt for sources, which would have more relevance to a history of medicine than to a study of rhetoric, I have cited some of the authorities most familiar to readers of the period without implying that the passages quoted are wholly original. I am more concerned with the rhetoric of writing about the female than about the male genitals, and more concerned with external appearances than with what might be observed in the anatomy theatre. The almost exclusively male writers were more curious about women's genital equipment than about their own familiar bodily parts. In an appendix I offer a brief summary of the more muted rhetoric found in practical handbooks for midwives, some of which were written by women.

The Latin words for the sexual organs, as used by anatomists and doctors of the early modern period, have in many cases somewhat different tonal qualities from those they had carried when used by classical poets, historians, letter writers, orators, and essayists. Indeed, it seems that in many cases the early modern writers used the Latin words as neutral synonyms, with little awareness of their earlier flavour. For their emotional and moral connotations in Roman society in classical times I am indebted to J. N. Adams, *The Latin sexual vocabulary*.

Although my interest extends to books written both in Latin and in the vernacular, I have found it useful to give some prominence to the second edition of Helkiah Crooke's *Μικροκοσμογραφία* (1631), which includes translations into English of a large proportion of the best known works in other languages.

In quotations from Latin, though not in titles, I have regularized by using *u* for *v* and *i* for *j*, by omitting diacritics, and by untying ligatures. Words written in the original treatises in Greek are printed here with the use of a basic Greek alphabet in which, regrettably, the circumflexes are unsightly. I have given the names of authors sometimes in their vernacular form, sometimes in the Latin, depending on which seems to be the more usual style of reference.

For advice I am grateful to Marion Halligan, Robin Hart, Lisa Miner, Kay Stevenson, and Brian Willis. For her unfailingly cheerful and intelligent assistance, I am grateful to Stella Clarke of the Rare Books Room in the Cambridge University Library.

RHETORIC AND DECORUM

Embarrassment, reticence, distress

In the preface to his comprehensive and popular Μικροκοσμογραφία,[1] Helkiah Crooke (1576-1635) excused himself for not having written in Latin, which he would have found easier, the terminology being ready to hand and the translation of quotations unnecessary. He says that to have done so would have "bin most ydle, my purpose being to better them who do not so well understand that language" (§3ʳ). He addresses himself in the first place to the worshipful company of barber-surgeons, many of whom were ignorant of Latin, and hopes that his work may serve as a textbook to help them improve their skills. Bearing his relatively humble readership in mind, he includes in the first paragraph of the preface to book iv, "Of the naturall parts belonging to generation, as well in men as in women" (197-256), an embarrassed apology for having to discuss the genitals. The length of the passage, together with its repetitive insistence, suggest that it may be read as rather more than a modesty topos:

> Being arived at this place in the tract of my Anatomicall Peregrination, I entred into deliberation with my selfe, whether I were best silently to passe it by, or to insist upon it as I had done in the former.[2] On the one side I conceived my labour would be but lame if it wanted this limbe, and a great part of my end and ayme frustrated, it being to exhibite the wonderfull wisedome and goodnesse of our Creator, which as in all the parts it is most admirable, so in this (if

---

[1] Helkiah Crooke, Μικροκοσμογραφία. *A description of the body of man* (1615) 2ⁿᵈ edn, enlarged (London 1631).

[2] Book 3: "Of the parts belonging to nutrition," in which he emphasizes, *inter alia*, the need to write of elimination (96).

perfection will admit any degrees) it is transcendent. The whole body is the Epitomie of the world, containing therein whatsoever is in the large universe; Seede is the Epitomy of the body, having in it the power and immediate possibility of all the parts. Moreover, the knowledge of these principles of generation is so much more necessary toward the accomplishment of our Art, by how much it is more expedient that the whole *kinde* should be preserved then any particular. Adde hereto, first that the diseases hence arising, as they bee most fearfull and fullest of anxiety especially in the Female sexe, so are they hardest to be cured: the reason I conceive to be, because the partes are least knowne as being veiled by Nature, and through our unseasonable modesty as it is called, not sufficiently discovered. Againe, the examples of all men who have undertaken this taske even in their mother tongues did sway much with me whose writings have received allowance in all ages and Commonwealths. On the contrary there was onely one obstacle, to reveyle the veile of *Nature*, to prophane her mysteries for a litle curious skilpride, to ensnare mens minds by sensual demonstrations, seemeth a thing liable to heavy construction. But what is this I pray you else but to Araigne Vertue at the barre of Vice? Hath the holy Scripture it selfe (the wisedome of God) as well in the old Law particularly, as also in many passages of the new, balked this argument? God that Created them, did he not intend their preservation, or can they bee preserved and not knowne? or knowne and not discovered? Indeede it were to be wished that all men would come to the knowledge of these secrets with pure eyes & eares, such as they were matched with in their Creation: but shall we therefore forfet our knowledge because some men cannot conteine their lewd and inordinate affections? Our intention is first and principally to instruct an Artist: secondarily that those who are sober minded might knowe themselves, that is, their owne bodies, as well to give glory to him who hath so wonderfully Created them; as also to prevent those imminent mischiefes to which amongst and above the rest these parts are subject. As much as was possible we have endevoured (not frustrating our lawfull scope) by honest wordes and circumlocutions to molifie the harshnesse of the Argument; beside we have so plotted our busines, that he that listeth may separate this Booke from the rest and reserve it privately unto himselfe. Finally, I have not herein relyed uppon my owne judgement, but have had the opinion of grave and reverent Divines, by whome I have bin perswaded not to intermit this part of my labour. My hope therefore is that my paynes in this part shall receive not onely a good construction, but also approbation and allowance of all those that are indeed wise. As for such as thinke there is no other principle of goodnesse then not to know evill, I would wish them to learne of their horses, that it is no good Mannage to stand stocke still but to move in order. We will apply our selves to our businesse. (197-98)

There follow five more paragraphs on the importance of perpetuating mankind, after which he steels himself in a final paragraph in preparation for attending to the relevant anatomical matters:

Againe, that there might bee a mutuall longing desire betweene the sexes to communicate with one another and to conferre their stockes together for the propagation of mankinde, beside the ardor and heate of the spirits conteyned in their seeds, the parts of generation are so formed, that there is not only a naturall instinct of copulation, but an appetite and earnest desire thereunto, and therefore the obscoene parts are compounded of particles of exquisite sense, that passion being added unto the will, their embracements might be to better purpose.[3] As for the

---

[3] Crooke's use of "obscoene," an adjective apparently out of keeping with his earlier positive remarks, may derive from his having here paraphrased a sentence from Laurentius and having failed to note the inappropriateness of the word in the context of his argument. If so, the failure is itself revealing. See below, 16-17, 18-19.

> particulars it shall be in vaine in this place to make mention of them, because the following discourse shall at large discipher them unto you. In which we will first describe the parts of generation belonging to men, and then proceede to those of Women also; of which wee would advise no man to take further knowledge then shall serve for his good instruction. And so we descend unto our history. (199)

The idea of descent in the last sentence suggests both that after some delay he braces himself for action and that the work involved will lead him into dark and earthy areas.

His nervousness soon returns. Halfway through his first chapter he again apologizes:

> Well, the History of these parts of generation it is our taske in this Book to describe, over which also we could wish we were able to cast a veile, which it should bee impiety for any man to remoove, who came not with as chaste a heart to reade as wee did to write. Howsoever, that which must needs be done, shal be done with as little offence as possible we may. (200)

At the end of his chapters on the male genitals, in which he touches very lightly on copulation, Crooke reverts to his apologetic manner:

> And thus much shall suffice for the parts of Generation in men, wherein I have bin indeed as particular as the Anatomicall History did require, but yet withall hope I shal finde pardon, because the Reader may perceive (at lest if he have any knowledge) that I have pretermitted many secrets of Nature, which I could and would heere have somewhat insisted upon, if I had imagined that al into whose hands this work should come had bin competent and fit auditors for such kinde of Philosophy. (216)

Such excuses had long been normal in anatomical treatises. In his famous and splendidly produced *De humani corporis fabrica*, on which so many later anatomists drew, Andreas Vesalius (1514-64) expressed some doubt as to whether he should embark on these delicate matters. While much briefer than Crooke's apology, the passage is more personal than is common in Vesalius's book.[4] He clearly means what he writes; the general tenor adopted by Crooke suggests that he too was sincere, if only because of nervousness as to his book's reception. It is, however, by no means clear how much real concern for the reader's blushes motivated the later authors and editors of more popular works such as *Aristotle's masterpiece* a handbook for midwives faintly pornographic in some versions. The preface to the account of the female genitalia in a well known edition published in 1704 begins with a decidedly more perfunctory apology:

> Was it not for the benefit of Practitioners and Professors of the Art of Midwifry, I should above all things spare to treat of these particulars, because they may be turned by some Lascivious and lewd Persons into ridicule, but they being absolutely necessary to be known, I will hope the best, and proceed in order.[5]

While many writers routinely apologize for offending modesty or even decline to speak in detail of the genitals,[6] Crooke would have wished for less constraint on the discussion of sexual matters: "our unseasonable modesty as it is called." Unseasonable is nevertheless a problematical word to use when addressing a Christian readership. Crooke asks "shall we therefore forfet our knowledge because some men cannot conteine their lewd and inordinate affections?" Some would say—still do say—Yes; he himself has omitted some details for just that reason. The book of Genesis seems to suggest that after the fall bodily modesty became and remained seasonable. Indeed, Crooke later contradicts himself once more when he mentions "*Coitus* or coition, that is, going together, A principle of Nature whereof nothing but sinne makes us ashamed" (258). Although the

---

[4] *De humani corporis fabrica* (Basileae 1543) 520-21.

[5] (1684) (London 1704) 96.

[6] Among them John Banister (see below, 19-20).

relevant sin is in the first place concupiscence—lewd and inordinate affections—Crooke implies that misuse of the anatomist's professional expertise may also be a danger, corrupting not only the emotions but also the mind. He wishes to be humble, to take care not to profane the mysteries of nature by exhibiting "a litle curious skilpride." In a style foreshadowing that of Thomas Browne, he adds that "to ensnare mens minds by sensual demonstrations, seemeth a thing liable to heavy construction." In his concluding passage on the male genitals (216) Crooke's account of the relationship of sin, prurience, and knowledge is contorted. He commends the divine nature of the genitals and declares God's intention that we should both care for them and know them. Some pages earlier he had nevertheless suggested that knowledge of the genitals may lead to an awareness of evil: "As for such as thinke there is no other principle of goodnesse then not to know evill . . ."; "wee would advise no man to take further knowledge then shall serve for his good instruction" (198, 199).

There are further awkward expressions and contradictions in Crooke's opening pages. He will use not only "honest wordes" but also circumlocutions. Despite his plea for openness he says that he has arranged his book so that the chapter on the genitals may be separated from the rest and read privately. He is writing, he says, to better his humble readers, yet also, influenced no doubt by Genesis, attributes prior understanding to them: "the Reader may perceive (at lest if he have any knowledge) that I have pretermitted many secrets of Nature . . ." One may ask why he is writing at all if his readers are already aware. He tells us, furthermore, that "grave and reverent Divines" had persuaded him not to "intermit" that part of his labour.

A popularizer in the vernacular, Crooke admits in his preface that for the bulk of his material he has drawn on and translated into readily graspable terms the work of others, most of whom he names. As a consequence he was viewed by his more conservative colleagues as too outspoken; his passages on generation caused trouble and almost led to the book's being suppressed.[7] Even serious

---

[7] See C. D. O'Malley, "Helkiah Crooke, M. D., F. R. C. P., 1576-1648," *Bulletin of the history of medicine* 42.1 (January-February 1968) 1-18, esp.

anatomists, writing in Latin, sometimes preface their descriptions, presented in a matter of fact tone, with an excuse or apology for having to embark on delicate matters. Gabriello Falloppio (1523-62) begins with a long, elegant, circumlocutory sentence explaining the physical necessity for the existence of the genital organs:

Cum homo propter substantiam ex qua constat, quam naturalis calor continue depabulando ad extremum tandem uiuendi terminum necessario producit: cum inquam propter eius substantiam, quae corruptibilis erat, sempiternus esse non posset: natura idipsum in specie, quod in individuo assequi impossibile erat, assequi conata est: atque hoc quibusdam fabricatis organis, in utroque sexu, quorum beneficio homo generetur. In hominibus igitur seminalia uasa ob hanc rem emolita est, duo in extremo atque infimo uentre, in parte exteriori, extra peritonaeum locauit corpora glandulosa, rotunda, atque oblonga in paruorum ouorum figuram, testes siue testiculi dicti sunt . . .[8]

Since man, because of the substance of which he is made, which natural heat by a process of continuous attrition necessarily brings at last to the end of its life, since, I say, because of his substance, which was corruptible, he could not be everlasting, nature took pains to pursue in the species an aim which could not be pursued in the individual, which was to be achieved with certain created organs, in each sex, by means of which mankind might be generated. For this

---

7-8; Geoffrey Keynes, *The life of William Harvey* (Oxford 1966) 72-75; Jonathan Sawday, *The body emblazoned* (London and New York 1995) 225-26. For a number of other reasons Crooke was in any case in bad odour with the College.

[8] Gabriello Falloppio, *Institutiones anatomicae* in *Opera genuina omnia* 3 vols (Venetiis 1606) I.8. While Falloppio clearly uses *peritoneum* in its modern sense, other writers of the period sometimes use it to mean *perineum*.

reason at the bottom and lower end of the belly in men it created seminal vessels; on the outside of the peritoneum it placed two bodies, glandular, round, and oblong, and having the shape of small eggs, called testes or testicles . . .

Both then and now, such rhetoric seems designed to defuse objections by implicitly acknowledging that this is nothing more than a decorous reformulation of what is already known. The tone is flat, with a careful avoidance of emphasis. Falloppio writes well; to some degree he nevertheless shares the common tendency—most pronounced, perhaps, in Crooke—to be loquacious in proportion to his sense of discomfort. As in the case of schoolroom lessons about delicate matters, boredom is likely to be the most common response to lengthy deadpan statements of the obvious.

The vulva

Medical writers usually reveal greatest embarrassment when the need arises to treat of women's genitalia. It is above all the appearance of the vulva, rather than its anatomical function, that causes disquiet. The frequent use of phrases such as "the obscene parts" may owe something to the etymology of the word "obscene." Although its derivation is unclear, it may be related to Latin *scaena*, suggesting that an obscene thing, *ob-scaenum*, is that which may be too readily exposed (on stage). In his book on gynaecology, Ludovicus Bonaciolus (late fifteenth century) had found himself troubled when describing the vulva, distressed both by the need to contemplate the female genitals and by the diction commonly applied to them. He implicitly appeals to the primacy of sight on the scale of moral worth: sight, the noblest of the senses, is easily distressed; by contrast, the meanest of the senses, touch (often used as a metaphor for sexual contact—e.g., *uirgo intacta*), is readily pleased by ignoble stimulation. Referring to the situation of the vulva between the thighs he asks rhetorically if there are any who do not know that, even though it is judged to be horrible to look at, disgusting to the sight, it stimulates powerful desire when touched:

In hac quoque parte uerenda atque femoribus Ueneris sedem poni in aperto est: pudendae nanque partis attrectatione, uehementem excitari libidinem quem latet? Haec adeo aspectu horrenda, obscoenaque uisu censetur . . .[9]

Although the question is general, and although mediaeval and renaissance commentators frequently repeat Avicenna's reminder that women may be given pleasure by stimulation of the clitoris,[10] there is little doubt that here Bonaciolus has only the response of men in mind. In contrast with its power to arouse the libido, he stresses the revolting appearance of the vulva, repeating the old belief that drowned women float prone, as if nature wished to preserve modesty by concealing the genitals, while men, who do not need to conceal theirs, float supine:[11]

. . . uti defunctarum etiam foeminarum cadauera (earundem alioquin pudori parcente natura) prona fluitent, quando uirorum contra supina, quippe quorum natura prona haud pudea. (664)

Perhaps wishing to pay no further attention to this subject he immediately passes to a specious series of physical explanations for the supposed facts.

Such profound disgust remained common among the anatomists. The English translator of Ambroise Paré (*c.* 1510-90), Dr Thomas Johnson, wrote pungently, modifying the language of the original and heightening it by adding lexical doublets and synonyms:

---

[9] Ludovicus Bonaciolus *Muliebrium libri II* (late 15th century) in Caspar Wolf, ed., *Gynaeciorum . . . libri veterum ac recentiorum* (Basileae 1566) cols 553-770, esp. II.i, col. 664.

[10] Avicenna, *Liber canonis* (11th century) trans. Gerard of Cremona (Basileae 1556) III, fen xxi, tract 1, chap. 10 (p. 711): *Ille enim locus, est locus delectationis eius.*

[11] The idea, very old, turns up frequently in mediaeval and renaissance discussions of *pudeur*.

out of all doubt unlesse nature had prepared so many allurements, baits, and provocations of pleasure, there is scarce any man so hot or delighted in venereous acts, which considering and marking the place appointed for humane conception, the loathsomnesse of the filth which daily falleth downe unto it, and wherewithall it is humected and moistened, and the vicinity and neerenesse of the great gut under it, and of the bladder above it, but would shun the embraces of women. Nor would any woman desire the company of man, which once premeditates or forethinkes with her selfe on the labour that she shall sustaine in bearing the burthen of her childe nine moneths, and of the almost deadly paines that she shall suffer in her delivery.[12]

Other versions of the passage continued to appear. Andreas Laurentius (d. 1609) writes of the genitals in highly charged, negative language, almost revelling, like Johnson, in the rhetoric with which he describes what he deems to be sordid sexual behaviour. If man were immortal his natural sense of revulsion at the female pudenda would ensure that he would never engage in the act of generation. Nothing but the power of sexual desire can overcome that revulsion in fallen man. In his view, modesty seems to be in no sense unseasonable:

> Hinc obscoenarum partium titillatio & sensus exquisitissimus. Quis enim per Deum immortalem concubitum rem adeo foedam solicitaret, amplexaretur, ei indulgaret? Quo uultu diuinum illud animal plenum rationis & consilii, quem uocamus hominem, obscoenas mulierum partes tot sordibus inquinatas, & ea rationi in locum imum uelut sentinam corporis relegatas attrectaret?

---

[12] Ambroise Paré, *Of the generation of man* (1586) in *The workes*, trans. Thomas Johnson (London 1634) 887. For the plainer original of Paré the practical man, see *Les oeuvres* (Paris 1628) 911-12.

Hence the titillation and most exquisite sensitivity of the obscene parts. For who, made immortal by God, would indulge that so filthy coital act, would embrace it, would take pleasure in it? With what countenance would that divine animal filled with reason and good counsel, whom we call man, touch the obscene parts of women, defiled with so much filth and for that reason relegated to the lowest part of the body, as if to the bilge?

What woman, he continues, would consent to sexual intercourse resulting in painful and possibly fatal labour, to be followed by the difficulty of nurturing a baby, *nisi incredibili uoluptatis oestro percita essent genitalia* (if the genitals were not violently stimulated by such an incredible arousal of desire).[13]

Others were less courageous than Bonaciolus, less inclined to rant than Laurentius. In the final paragraph of book vi of *The historie of man* (London 1578), "of the instrumentes servyng to the propagation of mankynd," John Banister wrote exclusively about the male

---

[13] Laurentius, *Anatomia humani corporis* (Parisiis 1600) 338. These passages in Paré and Laurentius are paraphrases and developments of Avicenna, III.20.16. The idea that only irresistible pleasure would cause a woman to engage in sexual intercourse was a commonplace of the period. See, for example, Crooke, *Μικροκοσμογραφία* 287. Sexual pleasure was sometimes thought to be necessary for impregnation. See Michael Dalton, *The countrey justice, conteyning the practise of the justices of the peace out of their sessions* (London 1618). Speaking of evidence concerning cases of rape, and citing authorities, he says: "If the woman at the time of the supposed rape, doe conceive with child, by the ravishor, this is no rape, for a woman cannot conceive with child, except she do consent" (248). Similar comments may be heard in modern times. *The Atlanta constitution* (21 April 1995) A18, reports Henry Aldridge, a dentist and Republican representative from North Carolina, as having made an anacoluthic assertion that victims of rape cannot be impregnated: "The facts show that people who are raped—who are truly raped—the juices don't flow, the body functions don't work and they don't get pregnant. . . . To get pregnant, it takes a little cooperation . . . and there ain't much cooperation in a rape." One may hope that he knew more about dentistry than he did about gynaecology.

genitals, declining to describe the vulva for fear of the possible effect such a passage might have "on the common sort":

> because I am from the begynnyng perswaded, that, by liftyng up the vayle of Natures secretes, in womens shapes, I shall commit more indecencie agaynst the office of *Decorum*, then yeld needefull instruction to the profite of the common sort, I do here ordaine the vi. rest of these my labours. (88ᵛ)

Although such expressions of aesthetic and moral distaste are frequent, passages of praise for the genitals, both male and female, are not uncommon. In the 1590s Gaspar Taliacotius (Gaspare Tagliacozzi, 1545-99), one of the pioneers of plastic surgery, wrote a sober book devoted to techniques for grafting skin and flesh to damaged parts of the face and head. Writing, in his introductory sections, of the beauty and elegance of the human face he found that the highest praise he could offer was to assert that it was still more beautiful than the genitals:

> *Sunt autem in maribus aeque, ac foeminis partes genitales, ea ratione dispositae, ubi locus cum ad sperma reiiciendum, recipiendumque, tum ad foetus incrementum, atque exenim omnium est aptissimus, qua neque sensuum operationes, neque mentis officia interpellari, neque splendor ille pulchritudinis obtenebrari potest. Quae omnia in faciei praestantiam eiusque dignitatem manifesto cedunt.*[14]

> There are in males, as also in females, genital parts, disposed in such a way that the place both for the ejection and receipt of sperm and for the growth of the foetus and for everything associated therewith is most fitting, and where that beauteous splendour can be neither harmed nor darkened by the operation of the senses or the activity of the mind. All

---

[14] Gaspar Taliacotius, *De curtorum chirurgia per insitionem* (Venetiis 1597) I.11.

of which matters clearly yield to the excellence and dignitie of the face.

Another writer of the same period, more circumspect than Taliacotius and writing in praise of women generally, implicitly denied that their sexual parts need be thought of as *pudenda*:

> . . . the exquisite proportion of sweet feminie [*sic*] bodies, is much more rare composed then those of men are, by judgement of the very best maysters in depth of skill: not making deniall of any one part, but that all doe aboundantly expresse the true celestiall measures.[15]

Crooke celebrates the Creator's work in respect of the genitals by calling it not only "perfection" but even "transcendent." Appealing to its vulnerability, he commends knowledge of it "especially in the Female sexe." Calling on scripture, he insists on the divine origin of the sexual parts. The more divine, however, the more fragile: he comments that diseases the "most fearfull and fullest of anxiety" are those that afflict the female genitals.

Theologians, philosophers, poets, artists, and some medical writers, almost always men writing for men, occasionally give evidence of a prurient interest in the female genitals even when they are adduced as a cynosure to remind us of our fallen nature. Although the relaxed penis was, at least until before the Council of Trent, openly represented by painters and sculptors, the female genitalia were, except in the most intimate circumstances, largely hidden from view and rarely depicted in detail in art. The frequent

---

[15] *An other defence of womens vertues, written by an honorable personage of great reckoning in Fraunce*, appended to *A womans woorth, defended against all the men in the world. Prooving them to be more perfect, excellent and absolute in all vertuous actions, then any man of what qualitie soever*, a translation, perhaps by Anthony Munday, of Alexandre de Pont-Aymeri's *Paradoxe apologique, ou il est fidellement démonstré que la femme est beaucoup plus parfaite que l'homme en toute action de vertu* (Paris 1594) (London 1599) 63[r].

covering of the female pubic hair by a scallop shell is a visual pun dependent on the Greek and Latin words κτείς and *pecten* which mean a comb and also (because of their similar shapes) both a scallop shell and the female pubis. To cover the pubis with a scallop is therefore both to disguise it and to draw attention to it by presenting a rebus.

Just as much bawdy talk today is stimulated by curiosity, so it was in the renaissance. In the prologue to his English version of Eucharius Roesslin's *Der swangern Frawen und Hebammen Rosegarten* (Strasburg 1512?), Thomas Raynalde pleads for a soberminded audience. Because of the startling nature of what he describes, some ribald and sexually ignorant men may experience a mixture of fear and prurience. Their reading of the book may move them, he says, "to abhor and loath the company of Women, and further in their communications to jest and bourd of Womens privities, not wont to be known of them . . . And if the knowledge of such things which commonly be called the womans privities, should diminish the heartie love and estimation of a woman in the mind of man, then by this reason, Physicians and Chirurgians wives should greatly be abhorred and misbeloved of their Husbands: and I my self likewise, which writeth this Book, should marvellously above many other abhorre or loath women; but to be short, there is no such thing, neither any cause thereto why."[16] Men—and, indeed, women also—are often reported, even in modern times, to have remained in ignorance of the structure of the female genitals after years of cohabitation.

Creative artists and doctors were sometimes willing to admit that a combination of curiosity and lust may lead men to wish to see the female genitals and to delight in what they find. The point is made in the opening scene of Marlowe's *Edward II* when Gaveston, describing the life of luxury with which he aspires to surround Edward and himself, imagines a courtly masque:

---

[16] The passages are taken from the "4th edn" (London 1654) 8, 12, of *The birth of mankind*, which is Thomas Raynalde's augmented version (first published 1545) of Richard Jonas's translation of the Latin version, *De partu hominis* (1532), of Roesslin's book. It was reprinted many times.

Like *Syluan* Nimphes my pages shall be clad,
My men like Satyres grazing on the lawnes,
Shall with their Goate feete daunce an antick hay.
Sometime a louelie boye in *Dians* shape,
With haire that gilds the water as it glides,
Crownets of pearle about his naked armes,
And in his sportfull hands an Oliue tree,
To hide those parts which men delight to see,
Shall bathe him in a spring . . .[17]

While the reference is in the first place to the female genitals, further innuendoes are contributed by the homosexual Gaveston's reminder to the audience that the role of Diana, goddess of chastity and punisher of male voyeurs, will be played by a "louelie boye."

In Bernard Mandeville's lighthearted, titillating lyric "On Celia's bosom" the change of taste separating Elizabethan and rococo times is revealed by a shift in decorum as the disguise inherent in Gaveston's masque is replaced by a more openly salacious use of classicism. Seeming at first to be another of the countless poems praising the female breasts, it proceeds to celebrate the woman in less familiar ways. The poem is neatly constructed in two parts, the two stanzas of sixteen lines each corresponding several times line for line in a series of amusing antitheses. Displaying and evidently enjoying his technical skill, Mandeville establishes almost mechanical polarities: cold and heat, soul and body, white and red, outer and inner, upper and lower.

On Celia's bosom

I

Ye Gods! how is my Soul amazed,
Since I on *Celia's* Bosom gazed;

---

[17] Christopher Marlowe, *The tragedy of Edward II* (1594) I.i.58-66, ed. C. F. Tucker Brooke (Oxford 1910) 315.

I saw the *Pink* and *July*-Flower,
Decay and Fade in half an Hour.
Wrapt up in wonder, when I spied   5
How soon the freshest Nosegays died;
By her Coldness, Mien and Dress,
By her Looks I thought no less,
But that the Flowers which were lost,
Were ruin'd by some nipping Frost;   10
Then looking on the modest Maid,
I bless'd her Innocence, and said,
Those Breasts are sure the *Pyrenean* Hills,
Where ev'n in *June*, a rigid Winter dwells;
And why the more I thought them so,   15
Was, that they look'd like deck'd with Snow.

II

But when I touch'd th'inviting Skin,
What Furnaces I found within;
I felt her Blood start up and fly,
And in her Veins boil Mountain high;   20
The Flame dispers'd thro' every part,
Shot thro' my Hand, and scorch'd my Heart.
Outward coldness is deceit,
And undone my mystick heat;
I'm like a Flower of Leaves bereft,   25
Where nothing but the Stalk is left;
What ever Snows without appear,
I'm sure there's a Ves[u]vious near.
And yet I'm tempted with a strong desire,
To go in quest of this deep Gulph of fire;   30
And will whatever place it is,
Like *Pliny*, venture on th' Abyss.[18]

---

[18] Bernard Mandeville, *Wishes to a godson, with other miscellany poems*
(London 1712) 16-18.

The parallelism of the poem's two parts is emphasised by Mandeville's handling of metre. While iambic tetrameter dominates, the second last couplet of each stanza is written in iambic pentameter, establishing a clear, repeated cadence. In the first stanza the lover sings of his having been overcome by the sight of the bosom of the celestial mistress. Her breasts do not, however, warm him and the world with their beauty. They are so cold that they wither the flowers of summer. Celia is perceived as a mountainous landscape which even in the hot climate of southern Europe is covered with snow.

The second stanza moves from sight to touch as the lover realizes that the snow-covered mountains are volcanoes. The realization does not, however, result in a conventional new burgeoning of the flowers with which he now explicitly identifies himself. Instead, he reimagines his ruined state: the withering of the flowers of superficial love leaves behind the stalk of sexual desire. With this new awareness he will go in quest of the source of erotic fervour, seeking out the female genitalia, "this deep Gulph of fire" (30). He pretends to be sexually innocent, ignorant of the nature of the place that he seeks. The conventional search for erotic satisfaction is transformed in the last lines into a desire for the satisfaction of sexual curiosity. He reveals implicitly that in the first place his desire is to observe and understand the mystery of Celia's female nature: Pliny the Elder died when watching and jotting scientific notes about the eruption of Vesuvius in 79 AD. Like Pliny, Mandeville's speaker will quest and venture further than may be safe, seeming at least as much interested in exposing hidden knowledge as in the act of physical penetration itself. The eruption of the sexual volcano is brought about by the lover's touch: "when I touch'd th'inviting Skin/ . . . I felt her Blood start up and fly/ And in her Veins boil Mountain high" (17-20). His "mystick heat" (24), a response to her apparent outward coldness, has been dispelled by her bodily heat, which he has both discovered and generated. Despite the suggestion that the encounter is headed toward physical union, the poem ends with a metaphor of voyeurism. However lifethreatening the dangers posed by vigorous female sexuality, the lover will stare at the vulva, simulating the curiosity of the naturalist, and perhaps, like Pliny, writing notes about what he observes. Mandeville expects to take pleasure in what he sees, however fearful and threatening it may seem. His readiness to describe the vulva to other men implies that they, too, are eager to look, if only in the imagination.

Also in the early eighteenth century a medical doctor, John Marten, confirmed both Marlowe's and Mandeville's poetic expressions of male sexual prurience, stating from his own experience that sexual curiosity leads men to take pleasure in watching female dissections. Although his introduction of a discussion of the female genitals lacks eloquence it is decidedly positive, praising their practical value, interest for the mind, emotional force, and aesthetic appeal:

> As Man . . . was by the great Creator most curiously made, and the Structure of his Parts in the most exquisite Order contriv'd; so Woman, and her Parts ministring to Generation, are no less admirable in every respect, as we shall by and by shew, in giving a Description thereof; and unless we enquire as particularly into the Parts of Woman, as we have of Man, we cannot come to the distinct Knowledge of the business of Generation.
>
> The Parts of a Woman that are calculated for that Office, are very curious and very useful, and as every Man's Passion is inflamed at the sight of them, so every curious Man is desirous of their being treated upon, being willing to know where and how he was form'd. When a Man at any time is Dissected, the place of Dissection is not so crouded, but when it happens to be a Woman, the Spectators would willingly be more numerous, did not Modesty in those concern'd forbid it, in turning away the Croud, as not worthy of the Sight, which is called, and that justly enough, pretty and fine.[19]

---

[19] John Marten, *Gonosologium novum: or, a new system of all the secret infirmities and diseases, natural, accidental, and venereal in men and women* (London 1709). Appended to the sixth edition of his *A treatise of all the degrees and symptoms of the venereal disease in both sexes* (London 1708?) 63 [misnumbered 62].

While it seems likely that the responses of the spectators were usually much as Marten reports, there is no hint of anything similar in Vesalius, who describes not only the human body, but also the methods he used to demonstrate his findings to an audience. In the section on the dissection of the female genitals, he gives no indication that the observers show any added curiosity about these matters.[20] That such dissections nevertheless generated intense interest is indicated by the famous illustration on the title page, where many observers watch intently as a female body is opened. Handbooks were available to assist the understanding.[21] In a preface "To the Courteous Reader," Alexander Read (1586?-1641) recommends his Σωματογραφία, a compendium from Crooke, to the attention of "him who onely by desultory inspection, laboureth to delight himselfe," and comments that it is simply laid out, clear, and portable, so that the curious viewer may take it to dissections "where the collation of the Figures, with the Descriptions, cannot but affoord great contentment to the minde."[22]

Names, circumlocutions, etymologies

Except for his initial apology at having to deal with matters of generation, Vesalius, who wrote with plain sobriety, was little concerned either with rhetoric or with the many variations in the nomenclature of the genitals, to which he briefly alludes (520). Nor does he devote more than passing attention to external appearances. In the anatomical works of other writers caution, reticence, and embarrassment were nevertheless commonly coupled, as often still today, with intense interest expressed in large numbers of graphic synonyms with varying affect. As both the writers and their intended

---

[20] Andreas Vesalius, *De humani corporis fabrica* (Basileae 1543) 557-58.

[21] For a discussion of the public response to theatres of anatomy, see Sawday, *The body emblazoned.*

[22] Alexander Read, Σωματογραφία ανθροπίνε, *or a description of the body of man* (1616) (London 1634) [A3ʳ⁻ᵛ]. The first edition is a compendium of Crooke's first (1615), while the second is a compendium of Crooke's expanded second (1631).

readers were almost without exception men, the female genitalia were less familiar than the male. The penis and testicles were readily observed;[23] by contrast, a woman's sexual equipment was largely hidden and mysterious. Some writers list synonyms for the penis, as numerous as those in any slang dictionary of the present day; many more give their fullest attention to the female sexual organs, a dozen or more parts being sometimes identified, with several names for each.[24]

As Bonaciolus spoke and read Latin every day in scholarly contexts, that language provided insufficient psychological and emotional distance when he considered the rich variety of ordinary Latin words for the vulva, which he calls *obscoena res*. Aware that the Greeks were said to have expressions which could be more tolerably uttered, he lamented the immoderate use of the more common and more unseemly terminology in the writings and pronouncements of virtually all the doctors of his day. He rejected popular derivations of vulva both from *ualua porta* (leafdoor: see below) and from *uolendo*,

---

[23] In writing *De pene* in his *De re anatomica libri xv* XI.xv (Venetiis 1559), Realdus Columbus says that although the penis is worthy of study, its shape is very familiar to all but eunuchs and the purblind. He adds, perhaps with a hint of irony, that its situation on the male body is very well known indeed: *Eius figura non modo uel eunichis ipsis, & lippis notissima est; situs item notissimus* (239). Laurentius writes: *Huius situs nulli non cognitus est* (342). In a major source book for later anatomists, *Institutiones anatomicae in Opera genuina omnia* 3 vols (Venetiis 1606) I.10, Falloppio says that the shape of the penis needs no description. (See below, 47.) In his *Lexicon physico-medicum: or, a new physical dictionary* (London 1719) John Quincy, M. D. (d. 1723), comments similarly but more succinctly, saying that its "Shape and Dimensions are pretty well known" (168). In his *Corporis humani anatomiae liber primus . . . secundus* 2nd edn (Bruxellis 1710) Philip Verheyen writes *Numerus, figura extrinseca, & situs cuilibet nota sunt* (I.114). Cf. also Vesalius: *Testium . . . in uiris situs nulli non conspicuus est* (521).

[24] Similar analyses may be found in recent times: "According to [Dr Irwin] Goldstein, a British researcher 'has identified 12 individual organs in female sexual function, most of which we'd never heard of'." *Modern maturity* (March/April 2001) 90.

eo quod insatiabiliter coitum uelit, atque desideret (ut uulgus retur)
(wishing, because it has an insatiable wish and longing for coitus, as
common people suppose). More than a vulgarity, this point,
repeatedly made in accounts of women's supposed lascivious
character and unruly genitals, was often supported by appeal to the
Vulgate version of Proverbs 30.15-16: *Tria sunt insaturabilia . . .*
Infernus, et os uuluae, et terra quae non satiatur aqua (There are
three insatiable things: . . . The abode of the dead, the mouth of the
womb, and the earth which is not saturated with water).[25] Despite the
difficulties of decorum Bonaciolus was not deterred, since he had
determined that he would include virtually everything in an
enterprise undertaken for decent reasons.[26] The passage is awkward
and troubled, revealing more real anxiety than Crooke was to do
more than a century later.

Although the Danish anatomist Caspar Berthelsen Bartholin (1586?-
1641) was dependent on earlier gynaecological treatises, his works—
those published during his lifetime together with those edited and

---

[25] The AV has "the barren womb." A more accurate rendering is "the
closing of the womb." See the Rev. Dr A. Cohen, *Proverbs: Hebrew text
and English translation with an introduction and commentary* (Hindhead
1945) 204.

[26] Bonaciolus, *Muliebrium libri II* col. 662: *Principio autem concinna serie,
contemplatione hac nobis pars illa, quam pudendam appellant, tractanda
sese ingerit offertque: quae non uel a ualua porta, uel a uolendo, eo quod
insatiabiliter coitum uelit, atque desideret (ut uulgus retur) quantum mea
fert opinio, uulua uocanda est. at eam paulo altius (ut perpensio haec
barbarorum offensam deprecetur) rerum luce repetita, pandendam duximus:
quando nihil quidem mihi unquam potius fuerit, quam ut huiusce obscoenae
rei & singulas partes, & Latina illarum quaeque nomina aperirem, quarum,
ut aiunt, apud Graecos uoculae & tolerabilius se habent, & acceptae iam
usu sunt: at obsoletiora foedioraque apud nos omnium ferme medicorum
uolumine famineque uerba insolentius iactitantur, ne uerecundius quidem
loquentium assuetudine quapiam commendata.*

   *Quo fit ut explanatio haec, & pudorem simul, & artis praecepta
seruantibus, difficilis euadat. Neque tamen ea res a scribendo me deterrere
debuit, quandoquidem hoc mihi curae fuerit, ut uel omnia, quae frugi
accepi, comprehenderem.*

revised by his son Thomas (1616-80) and by his grandson Caspar
Thomasen (1655-1738)—were much cited and paraphrased as
authorities. Following some attention to the penis, Bartholin begins
his comments on the vulva with a gloss on the word, offering an
interesting list of synonyms, repeating terms in Bonaciolus but going
beyond them:

> . . . quasi ualua, item cunnus, a cuneo aut impressione forte
> dictus. Plauto saltus, hortus, fundus, alia item translatione,
> concha, & nauis eidem, aliis communiter natura muliebris.
> (153).

> . . . as if to say, a leafdoor; it is also called the cunt, from
> the word wedge or perhaps from the impression created by a
> wedge. In Plautus it is called a pasture, a garden, a farm, or,
> from another point of view, a mussel shell and a ship. In the
> work of others it is commonly called the female nature.[27]

---

[27] *Hortus* is not, in fact, so used in Plautus, but *hortulus* appears,
conjecturally, in the *Anthologia Latina*. See J. N. Adams, *The Latin sexual
vocabulary* 84.

At Emory University in Atlanta—and doubtless elsewhere in the United
States—medical trainees learning to interpret the language used by lay
people to describe their symptoms have been advised at least until recently
that a man suffering from impotence may complain of trouble with his
"nature." A common euphemism for the female genitals in classical times,
natura is also frequently found in that sense—both in Latin and in
translation—in the renaissance. *OED* records no use of the word in
reference to the penis, nor any use for the female genitals later than the
eighteenth century. The related use of the word to refer to the *menses*
continues to be found in modern times. The survival, in the southern United
States, of "nature" as a euphemism for the genitals is characteristic of
linguistic forms in former colonial territories. The origin of its use with
reference to the penis nevertheless warrants investigation. Information
received from Lisa Miner, who was a trainee physician's assistant in
Atlanta in 1995.

The Greeks also spoke of the female genitals in pastoral terms: κῆπος meant both garden and the vulva. These pleasing if also somewhat proprietory terms are rarely reflected in the rhetoric of early modern anglophone writers.

The suggestion, frequently repeated in the early modern period, that *uulua* is a transformation of *ualua*, a leafdoor, is a characteristic example of etymology by analogy, both orthographical and physical. Although the words are etymologically unrelated it is not difficult to see the attraction of the supposed derivation. The leafdoor suggests an analogy with the *labia maiora*, a barrier that may be either opened or locked giving or denying access to the *domus*, the feminine domain, a barrier that may be guarded by a male protector. Séverin Pineau (sixteenth to seventeenth centuries), who dwells at length on the shape, size, tension, humidity, and other immediate qualities of the vulva, glosses the etymology imaginatively, if also with comic solemnity and explicitness. He comments that it is easy to open the double door—conceived as that of some grand house—a phrase suggesting a positive if also nervous response to women's sexuality:

> *uulua uocetur . . . quia mediante rima amplissima in duas diuiditur partes, dextram uidelicet ac sinistram, quae clauduntur & aperiuntur, ut ualuae alicuius domus insignis, & ab inuicem, quando opus est, distrahuntur uel diducuntur aperienturue minimo negotio.*[28]

> It is perhaps called the vulva . . . because as a result of the great cleft it is divided into two parts—that is to say, the right and the left—which are closed and opened like the leafdoors of some grand house; when necessary they can

---

[28] Séverin Pineau, *De virginitatis notis, graviditate & partu* (1597) (Lugduni Batavorum 1650) 31. Later (68-69) Pineau contradicts himself when writing of the difficulty and pain of a man's gaining a first entry unless that is undertaken during the humidifying and relaxing period of menstruation or up to four days thereafter. In this discussion he is concerned only with the *labia maiora*. Impregnation was thought to occur soon after menstruation.

also, by turns, be separated or drawn apart or opened with the minimum of effort.

The history of the reception of the words *cunnus* and cunt is curious. Although cunt is frequently found in mediaeval English books of anatomy, it is avoided by later authorities who nevertheless regularly use *cunnus*, to which in their turn classical Latin speakers would have reacted with discomfort.[29] For them, *cunnus* was as grossly obscene a word as cunt is for many fastidious speakers of English in the present day.[30] Medical writers of the renaissance use *cunnus* with no sense of impropriety:

> The *clitoris*, or little prick in women, hath foure muscles. . . . The two lower are broad and smooth, and proceeding from the *sphincter* of the *anus*, are inserted into the brims of the *cunnus*.[31]

In the expanded editions of Bartholin published by his son Thomas further names were added with a hint of quiet humour:

> *Romanis porca apud* Uarronem. *Quo autem mordacitatis sensu* Suidas & Eustathius κύνειρον *seu* κύωνα *hoc est, canem uocauerint, iudicent experti.*[32]

The printer of the translation of Bartholin published by Culpeper and Cole in 1663 obscured the sense by his choice of punctuation:

> *Uarro* tells us the Romans called it *Porca* the Furrow or Parsley-bed, the Sow. And what Experience of biting made,

---

[29] See *OED2* for a mediaeval example of the use of cunt.

[30] See Adams 2, 9, 66, 80-81.

[31] Alexander Read, *A treatise of all the muscles of the body of man* (1637) in *The workes* 3rd edn (London 1659) 508.

[32] Thomas Bartholin, *Anatomia, ex Caspari Bartholini parentis institutionibus . . . reformata* (Hagae-Comitis 1655) 182.

[punct. *sic*] *Suidas* and *Eustathius* call it *cuneiron* or *cuona*, the Dog, let those judg that can speak by Experience.[33]

There are two Latin words *porca*, etymologically unrelated. One means the ridge between two furrows; English furrow and Latin *porca* derive from the same root. The other means a sow. Culpeper and Cole evidently take both meanings to be relevant. They are right. Perhaps deriving from a variant edition, Bartholin's *porca*, sow, is a change of the text usually found in Varro, who speaks of *porcus*, a male pig. He says that Latin women, especially nurses, used the word to refer to the genitals of young girls (the quality of nature which makes them women), and that Greek women called it by the equivalent Greek word, χοῖρος. By this they indicated that the pig was a worthy symbol of marriage since it was given by nature to be eaten at a banquet just as life was given to the pigs, like salt, to preserve their flesh:

> *nostrae mulieres, maxime nutrices, naturam qua feminae sunt in uirginibus appellant porcum, et graecae choeron, significantes esse dignum insigne nuptiarum. Suillum pecus donatum ab natura dicunt ad epulandum; itaque iis animam datam esse proinde ac salem, quae seruaret carnem.*[34]

The Greek words based on κύων, dog or bitch, have, in this context, little to do with biting; their sexual applications are, however, complex. The word κύων can itself mean the penis, the penial fraenum, and the female pudendum. The derivative κύνειρα (dogleash) and its variant κύνειρον are also applied to the vulva. In addition, the Greeks sometimes expressed shame, shamefulness

---

[33] Thomas Bartholin, *Bartholinus anatomy; made from the precepts of his father . . .* published by Nicholas Culpeper and Abdiah Cole (London 1663) 75.

[34] Varro, *De re rustica* II.iv.10.

(Latin *pudor, uerecundia*) by the use of words which might be translated as "dogishness."[35]

The ordinary Latin word for parsley and similar herbs is *apium*. By interpreting the furrow as a parsleybed Culpeper and Cole are not, however, referring to the Latin. They are, rather, invoking an old habit of nursery speech as explained in, for example, *The rogue*, the English translation of Alemán's *Guzmán de Alfarache*: "that phrase which we use to little children, when we tell them they were borne in their mothers Parsly-bed."[36] As they use it the parsleybed is thus no longer a pretty deflection of attention from the sexual organs but an imaginary transformation of the *labia maiora* and the pubic hair. In the same context, glossing *a cuneo aut impressione*, Culpeper (or Cole) adds an interesting parenthesis of his own: "*whence in a Manuscript of English Receipts, I have found it called* the Print" (74). This oddity (not recorded in *OED*) presumably arose from a translator's misunderstanding of *impressione*; the author of the manuscript would doubtless not have been surprised to find any word at all used as the name of a sexual organ.

In their opening paragraphs referring to the vulva in general anatomists continued to list further words. Regnerus de Graaf (1641-73) adds *larua*, an evil spirit or a horrible mask, perhaps deriving from the folk tradition that the female genitals, as in representations of the *sheela na gig*, are apotropaic. He also includes *scissura*, a crack or cleft, offering as possible explanation that the vulva causes splits and divisions among men, in support of which he quotes a line of Horace:

---

[35] See *Suidas*, the *Lexicon* of Stephanus (Henri Estienne), and Eustathius, commentary on *The Odyssey* XVII, 1821.51-56, 1822.13-16 (Odysseus and his dog Argos).

[36] Mateo Alemán, *Guzmán de Alfarache* (1599, 1604) trans. James Mabbe as *The rogue* (London 1623) I.25, marginal note. Mabbe misunderstands Alemán. His main text refers to a "Mellon-bed," translating Spanish *melonada*, which in this context means, rather, a silly mess (concerning paternity). See the edition published in Milan, 1603, 38. For other examples of the saying about birth in a parsleybed, see Morris Palmer Tilley, *A dictionary of the proverbs in England in the sixteenth and seventeenth centuries* (Ann Arbor 1950) B6.

> *fuit ante Helenam cunnus taeterrima belli*
> *causa* (*Serm.* I.iii.107-8)

> the cunt was a most terrible cause of warfare before Helen's
> time

Mentioning *porcus*, using the masculine form, he makes a comment
related to the passage in Varro: the Romans often sacrificed a pig at
weddings in the hope that the bride would be as fertile as a breeding
sow. Along with Varro he points out that the Greeks also called the
vulva the pig, χοῖρος. The word and its derivatives are indeed often
found in that sense—and in particular with reference to the hairless
vulva—in the Greek comic poets.[37]

Detailed and methodical descriptions of the female genitals, usually
starting from the outside and working in, are repeated from text to
text, the medical treatises often being quoted or paraphrased in
popular works designed as much for titillation as for instruction.
Writers commonly start by listing what can be seen without pulling
aside the labia before proceeding to what may be found when they
are separated. In the introductory statements of the most commonly
cited Latin authorities there occur two principal variants of the
phrase alluding to the separation of the labia. The more frequent of
the two is exemplified by Kaspar Bauhin:

> *aliae plane externae sunt, quae absque labiorum diductione*
> *se offerunt; aliae internae, quae non nisi facta labiorum*
> *digitis, in utrumque latus separatione, patent.*[38]

---

[37] Regnerus de Graaf, *De mulieribus organis generationi inservientibus* in
Opera omnia (Lugduni Batavorum 1677) 167-68. For an extended passage,
see Aristophanes, *The Acharnians* 739-49. A simple euphemism sometimes
seen is Latin *res*, "thing." See, for example, Michael Ettmüller, *Opera
omnia* (Lugduni 1685) II.422. Since the middle ages "thing" has been used
in English to mean a sexual organ.

[38] Kaspar Bauhin, *Theatrum anatomicum* (Francofurti 1605) 256.

some are fully external and appear without the pulling aside of the labia; others are internal and are not to be seen unless by means of the fingers the labia are opened sideways in either direction.

The alternative version is found in Laurentius:

aliae [*particulae*] *quidem statim obuiae etiam citra sectionem; aliae sub his latitantes. Obuiae sunt, pubes, monticulus, labra duo, magna rima; latitant autem sub his, alae & nymphae, carunculae quatuor, clitoris & urinae meatus.*[39]

some [parts] are indeed immediately to be seen without separation of the lips; others lie beneath those. Immediately visible are the pubis [or, the pubic hair], the mons, the *labia maiora*, the great cleft; under these there lie the wings and the *labia minora*, the four caruncles, the clitoris, and the urinary meatus.

That the female genitals were examined in obsessive detail is confirmed especially by the inclusion in the list of two words for the *labia minora* and of "the four caruncles," often described as myrtiform.[40] Although repeatedly mentioned, it seems that the caruncles, small protuberances said to surround the urinary meatus, existed as much in the imagination as in reality. The insecurity of their status is confirmed by Culpeper and Cole's having reversed the sense of Bartholin's last sentence. Where Bartholin writes

. . . *nec unquam conterentur, etiam in iis, quae saepissime coiuere aut peperere*

---

[39] Laurentius, *Anatomia humani corporis* 356.
[40] For example, Bartholin, *Anatomia* 183 and figure on 185 (misprinted 158). In *De re anatomica* Realdus Columbus attributes to the *labia minora* the function of keeping out dust, cold, and air (242). The physical distinction between the *labia minora* and the caruncles was often blurred.

> . . . nor do they ever wear away even in those who have
> frequently copulated or given birth

they translate:

> Their *Shape* resembles the Berries of Myrtle.
> Their *Size* varies, for some have them shorter, longer,
> thicker and thinner then others. Howbeit they abide til
> extream old Age and wear not away so much as in those that
> have used frequent Copulation and frequent Child-bearing.
> (75)

The supposed function of the caruncles was equally uncertain. They
might serve to close the mouth of the vagina to keep out dust and
cold air, offer a source of "titillation and pleasure, while they are
swollen, and strongly strain, and milk the Yard, as it were,
especially in young Lasses," or leave only a small opening in the
hymen.[41] Graaf confessed (192) that although they were much talked
of he could find nothing that warranted the name. They were, he
suggests, merely roughnesses and inequalities of skin at the mouth of
the vagina. At one point (237) Crooke calls a caruncle in the vulva a
"fleshy hillocke" but, perhaps because caruncle is a purely
anatomical word and concept, other labels are rare.

Use of the vernacular for a more popular audience continued to
cause some writers problems. In a splendidly indignant paragraph
Thomas Gibson (1647-1722) excused himself for having written in
English, saying that his motive was accuracy:

> to avoid the injury of a paltry Translator, if it should be well
> accepted. For we see there is no Man that publishes any
> thing in the Latin tongue, that is received with any applause,
> but presently some progging Bookseller or other finds out an
> indigent Hackney scribler to render it into English. But with
> what dis-reputation and abuse to the worthy Authors, every
> learned person cannot but observe. So that he that shall think

---

[41] Culpeper and Cole 75.

to redeem the noble faculty and art of Physick out of the hands of the Mechanical Quacking Tribe by publishing every thing in a language above their understanding, will not only fail of his end, but find himself abused and disgraced into the bargain.[42]

While Gibson's own latinity was perhaps secure other medical popularizers with an uncertain grasp of the language encountered difficulties. In the general descriptions of the external female genitalia, the phrases *absque* [or *sine*] . . . *diductione* and *citra sectionem* proved awkward. The first refers to what may be seen without digital interference. The second is more ambiguous. In many cases it means without surgical section; in classical Latin the first meaning of *sectio* is an act of cutting.[43] Later it also acquired the more immediately physical sense of a cut, section, or division. Laurentius means merely an act of separation. His use of balanced phrases leaves little doubt that what he intended was a distinction between the parts that may be seen without drawing back the sides of the cleft, the *labia maiora*, and those that lie hidden beneath them. Translators of these texts sometimes make nonsense of them or radically alter the sense, even when satisfactory English versions were already to be found in the medical literature. Rendering Bauhin's *absque . . . diductione*, Gibson got it right by using the technical term "diduction," rarely found outside anatomical and scientific treatises:

> The Parts that offer themselves to view without any diduction, are the *Fissura magna* or great chink, with its *Labia* or Lips, the *Mons Ueneris* and the Hairs. These parts are called by the general name of *Pudenda*, because when they are bared they bring *pudor* or shame upon a Woman. (156)

---

[42] Thomas Gibson, *The anatomy of humane bodies epitomized* (London 1682) (A3ᵛ-A4ʳ).

[43] For example Vesalius 528.

Repeating the passage almost verbatim in about 1708, John Marten, or his printer, transformed "diduction" into "deduction," a word with a different sense and derivation and with wholly new connotations. In place of a statement about what is exposed to view without uncovering any parts by the use of the fingers, Marten now appears to apologize for his boldness in omitting nothing from his list:

> The *Pudendum Muliebre* or Privities of Women, are next to be consider'd, and that which offer themselves to view without any deduction are the *Fissura Magna* or great Chink, with its *Labia* or Lips, the *Mons Ueneris*, and Hairs, which are called by the General Name of *Pudenda*, because when they are bared they bring *Pudor* or Shame upon a woman.[44]

Helkiah Crooke is one of many who, misreading the thrust of Laurentius's *citra sectionem*, established a false descriptive tradition that seemed to appeal, plausibly enough, to the process of dissection which will follow the examination of the parts to be observed both before and after the labia have been manually separated. An apology for openness is replaced by the objective, impersonal, clinical connotations of anatomy:

> In this there are many parts to be discerned without dissection. Of which some are altogether outward, offering themselves before the wings be displaied; others inward, not

---

[44] John Marten, *Gonosologium novum* 80. It also turns up in *Aristotle's masterpiece*, many versions of which, badly printed, reveal chaotic mistranslations and misunderstandings: "The parts that offer themselves to view, without any Deduction, at the bottom of the Belly are the *Fissura Magna*, or the Great Chink, with its *Libia* [*sic*], or Lips, the *Mons Ueneris*, and the Hair. These parts are called by the general Name of *Pudenda* because when they are bared they bring *Pudor*, or Shame upon a Woman" (1684) (London 1704) 96. That "chink" in this sense was in common use in Shakespeare's time is shown by, for example, the familiar *double entendre* of the chink in the wall through which Pyramus and Thisbe communicate in *A midsummer night's dream*. Thisbe's kissing of the "stones" adds a bawdy allusion to the male genitals (V.i).

appearing before the wings be opened and separated on both
sides. (237)

Crooke here seems to be offering a straight, though flawed,
translation of a version of Bauhin's passage in which Laurentius's
citra sectionem has replaced *absque . . . diductione*.

Alexander Read repeated Crooke's misreading of *citra sectionem*,
though in his case it seems that he had little idea what the sentence in
his source might mean: "*Cunnus* is that part which offereth itselfe to
the sight before section. In it eleven particles are remarkable."[45]
When he proceeds to discuss the *labia minora*, "the *Alae*, or
Nymphae, the wings," he reinforces the inappropriate clinical tone of
"section": "these appeare when the lips are severed" (120).
Although in the seventeenth century, as in the twentieth and the
twentyfirst, "sever" could mean simply "separate," use of the word
in an anatomical context potentially evokes the idea of work with the
scalpel.

A passage from Bartholin, once again starting with the word
diduco, takes the next step, describing what may be seen once the
labia have been separated:

> *Diductis labiis apparet 1. Magna fossa cum exteriori Rima
> magna, & eam fossam nauicularem uocare possumus: quia
> nauiculae figuram habet. Est enim retrorsum magis profunda
> & lata, ut inferior posteriorque finis tanquam in fossam
> degeneret.*[46]

> Once the labia have been separated there appears 1. The
> great embanked ditch with the great external fissure, and we
> can call that ditch shiplike since it has the shape of a little
> ship. Towards the rear it is in fact deeper and wider, as if
> the lower, more distant end were degenerating into a ditch.

---

[45] Alexander Read, *The manuall of the anatomy or dissection of the body of
man* (London 1612) 119.
[46] Caspar Berthelsen Bartholin, *Institutiones anatomicae* 153.

In classical Latin *fossa*, a ditch, had sometimes been used in unflattering contexts to refer to the vulva. The word is here used in the slightly different later Latin sense of an embanked ditch with built-up sides.[47] Translators had trouble with Bartholin's passage. Crooke used words suggesting once again that he was far from sure what was meant. He evidently hoped that if he rendered more or less literally his readers would understand something obscure to himself: "the more [the cleft] tendeth backward the deeper and broader it is, and so degenerateth into a trench or valley, representing the figure of a boate, and endeth in the welt of the orifice of the necke" (238). The Culpeper and Cole translation of Bartholin is still more contorted:

> . . . we may call the foresaid Ditch *Fossa nauicularis* the Boat trench, because of its likeness to a little Boat or Ship. For it is backwards more deep and broad, that the lower and after-end might degenerate as it were the Ditch or Trench.[48]

In the revised editions published after Caspar Berthelsen Bartholin's death, his son Thomas added a passage describing the venereal glands—"Bartholin's glands"—that later came to be associated with his own son Caspar Thomasen:

> *In illa fossa diductis labiis apparent duo foramina, sed fere tantum in uiuis, cum admodum parua sint, in quibus serosus quidam humor non parua quantitate prodit, qui maris pubem in coitu madefacit.*[49]

When the lips are separated there appear in this embanked ditch two openings—but almost only in living bodies, since they are very small—from which no small quantity of a

---

[47] Thomas Bartholin notices the similar connotations of *porca* as a slang word for the vulva. *Nauis* or *nauicula* are frequently used in classical literature to mean the vulva.

[48] Thomas Bartholin, *Bartholinus anatomy* 75.

[49] Thomas Bartholin, *Anatomia* 183.

certain serous humour pours forth, which wets the husband's private parts [or, pubic hair] during coitus.

Or, in the Culpeper and Cole version:

> In this Ditch the Lips being opened, two Holes appear, but hardly visible, save in live bodies, out of which a good quantity of wheyish Humor issues, which moistens the Mans Share in the time of Copulation. (75)

The image of the ship with reference to the outward appearance of the vulva fascinated many writers. In addition to ship or skiff, *nauicula* meant the nave of a church (shaped like an inverted ship); the conceptual nexus of female sexuality and divinity seems to be universal.[50] For a moment Pineau greatly strengthens the divine associations of the genitals, only to bring his diction quickly down to earth again:

> *uagina . . . nauiculae cuiusdam formam habet, unde pronaum praedictae rimae pars posterior & cutis quae eidem sinui aut nauiculae praeest, a nobis appellatur, necnon fossa, quia tanquam uallis est monticulis undique cincta.* (76)

> the vagina . . . has the shape of a kind of little ship, or nave, whence we call the rear part of the aforesaid cleft and skin which guards that hollow or nave a temple-portico and also an embanked ditch, since it is like a valley surrounded on all sides by hills.

Reworking this source material, Crooke is, as usual, loquacious and imprecise. He adds a further anatomical implication when he reads *ualua* according to another of its meanings: some, he says, call it "*Uulua*, as it were *uallis* a valley, or *Ualua* a Flood-gate, because

---

[50] See, for example, Clive Hart and Kay Gilliland Stevenson, *Heaven and the flesh* (Cambridge 1995) *passim*.

it is divided into two parts by a cleft, which like Flood-gates or leafe-doores are easily opened or shut as neede is." While physically consistent with the humidity of the vulva, the connotations of "flood-gate" suggest a very different relationship of the male observer to the female anatomy. He no longer imagines himself only as a visitor to a grand house, whose doors may be readily opened for his admittance, but also as a bystander watching the opening and closing of canal locks regulating liquid masses which, although under a man's control, are impersonal and suggest a vastly bigger scale of natural forces. Making a choice among alternative English words for the vulva, Crooke abandons the topographical metaphors and decides on a semi-euphemism: "We will call it the lappe." (237)

The parts, or "particles," to which most attention is given in more detailed descriptions of the female genitals are the *labia minora*, usually called *alae* (wings) or *nymphae* (nymphs), and the clitoris. Realdus Columbus lays great stress on Avicenna's frequently repeated remark about the importance of the clitoris as the locus of female pleasure, insisting, as many did, that without the pleasure derived from its stimulation no woman would ever consent to copulate (243). The clitoris was early understood to be the woman's equivalent of the penis, a point routinely made by the anatomists. The function of the *labia minora* as an independent entity proved more puzzling. Crooke calls them "a skinny addition of the neck . . . answering to the prepuce or foreskin of a man . . ." (237) and goes on to describe what he takes to be their function:

> These *Nymphae*, beside the great pleasures women have by them in coition, doe also defend the wombe from outward injuries, being of that use to the orifice of the necke which the fore-skin is to the yard; for they do not onely shut the cleft as it were with lips, but also immediately defend the orifice as well of the bladder as the wombe from colde aire and other hurtfull things. Moreover, they leade the urine through a long passage as it were betweene two walles, receiving it from the bottome of the cleft as out of a Tunnell: from whence it is that it runneth foorth in a broad streame with a hissing noyse, not wetting the wings of the lap in the

passage; & from these uses they have their name of
Nymphes, because they joyne unto the passage of the urine,
and the necke of the womb; out of which, as out of
Fountaines (and the *Nymphes* are sayed to bee presidents or
Dieties of the Fountaines) water and humors doe issue: and
beside, because in them are the veneriall delicacies, for the
Poets say that the *Nymphes* lasciviously seeke out the *Satyres*
among the Woods and Forrests. (237-38)

A century later John Marten included similar comments in his
anatomical summaries:

When the Chink is opened by drawing aside the *Labia* or
Lips, that which offer themselves next to our View are the
Nymphae or *Clitoris*. The *Nymphae* or Nymphs, or as others
Alae or Wings, are so called because they stand next to the
passage of the Urine on each side of it, and keep the Lips of
the Privities and Hair from being wet as the Urine spouts out
of the Bladder . . . they . . . are almost triangular, and . . .
for their Shape and Colour, being soft and red, are compared
to the Thrils that hang under a Cock's Throat. . . .
   We have already spoken of the use of the *Nymphae* to
defend the Urine from wetting the Lips, which they do, by
peculiarly guiding and turning strait the Stream of the
Womans Urine as it comes out of the Bladder, causing it to
make that hissing Noise as is observ'd when evacuated, and
which the shortness and width of the passage of Urine in
Women . . . and their squatting and forcing posture when
they make Urine, very much contributes to.[51]

As has been frequently discussed, Marten's conflation of the *labia
minora* and the clitoris was common—though by no means

---

[51] John Marten, *Gonosologium novum* 82, 83. The passage is largely a
recasting of Gibson 157-58. For Latin sources of these remarks see, for
example, Caspar Berthelsen Bartholin, *Institutiones anatomicae* (1611) new
edn (Goslariae 1632).

universal—in early modern descriptions of the female genitals.[52] Instead of identifying the parts individually, anatomists often spoke of the whole area as the locus of women's erotic pleasure. Graaf is scornful of the error.[53] Crooke shows signs of coyness when he attempts to explain the origin of the word clitoris. With the image of female homosexual behaviour in mind, he writes:[54] "*Clitoris* in Greeke κλειτορίς commeth of an obscoene word signifying contrectation, but properly it is called the womans yard." His etymology is at fault. The primary word is κλειτορίς on which are based κλειτοριάζο or κλειτορίζο meaning to touch the clitoris (contrectation). He reflects the horror felt by many men at the thought of hermaphrodism and female homosexual practices: "sometimes it groweth to such a length that it hangeth without the cleft like a mans member; especially when it is fretted with the touch of the cloaths, and so strutteth and groweth to a rigidity as doth the yarde of a man. And this part it is which those wicked women doe abuse called *Tribades* . . . to their mutuall and unnaturall lustes" (238).

Although commonly mentioned and briefly described, the hymen receives from the anatomists perhaps surprisingly little attention.[55] Its conventionally alleged usefulness in confirming virginity is cited. Perhaps because it had an inherently passive role and, once broken, served no further purpose, it nevertheless fails to capture the anatomists' imagination. Few alternative names are found. In one passage Crooke calls it "a skinny Ligament . . . or skinny tye" (236) but elsewhere in the text and in the figures he uses the familiar word. Graaf uses no other word than hymen.

---

[52] They are not conflated by Gibson, who has "the *Nymphae* and the *Clitoris*" (157).

[53] See *De mulieribus organis generationi inservientibus* 174.

[54] See, for example, Katharine Park, "The rediscovery of the clitoris: French medicine and the tribade, 1570-1620," in David Hillman and Carla Mazzio, edd. *The body in parts: fantasies of corporeality in early modern Europe* (New York and London 1997) 171-93.

[55] There are significant exceptions. Graaf devotes an entire chapter to it (*De hymene*, 188-207).

Still less attention is given to words for the pubic hair, sometimes mentioned as an emblem of modesty. It is usually called simply "hair"—or "the hairs," in Latin, *pili*. Neither the physical appearance nor the words appear to have stimulated the anatomists' linguistic inventiveness.

The further the anatomists penetrated into the woman's sexual parts the more extreme the imagery tended to become. Vesalius's etching of an excised vagina and uterus made to look like the negative of a penis, repeatedly recopied, has been frequently discussed.[56] Many anatomists of the later renaissance rejected the notion that the penis and the vagina were essentially similar, as they did the associated Aristotelian belief that a woman was an imperfect man. Graaf says that the idea *ridiculum plane est*, and that the vagina and the penis are in no sense alike.[57] Other comparisons of female genital parts are equally striking. In his passage on the uterus, Realdus Columbus tells his reader that if he were to examine the cervix his eyes would be met by something that looked like the head (or mouth) of a tench or dog [or, perhaps: like a tench or the head of a dog]: *si extra spectes, tinchae piscis, uel canini oris nuper in lucem editi imaginem tuis oculis offeret.*[58]

The penis, the testicles, the scrotum

When speaking of the male genitals anatomists commonly began, as they did with the female, by positing a distinction between inner and outer parts. Their discussion of the inner parts of the male genitalia is, however, quite different in tone. Because in this case there is nothing internal to be seen without surgical dissection, their accounts are simpler, more factual, less emotive. While there is some rhetorical interest in their discussion of what is externally visible, they nevertheless write with comparative brevity. Falloppio's

---

[56] Vesalius, *De humani corporis fabrica* 381. And see, for example, Sawday, *The body emblazoned* 221.
[57] *De mulieribus organis* 220. Bartholin (1665) is also dismissive (154).
[58] Columbus, *De re anatomica* 240.

avoidance of a detailed account of the penis, suggesting that it is unnecessary, was frequently repeated by later writers:

> penis . . . in cuius extremo glans appellata collocatur: in hanc desinit uirile pudendum, cuius figura magis nota est, quam ut descriptione explicari egeat: eius substantia ex simpliciori ac delicatiori carne constat, ac maxime sensili.[59]

> the penis . . . at the extremity of which the part called the glans is to be found: this is where ends the male pudendum whose shape is better known than to need explanation by means of a description: its substance consists of flesh that is very simple and delicate, and highly sensitive.

In a characteristically sober passage on the penis, Caspar Berthelsen Bartholin declines to list common words for it: *communiter* Penis *dicitur, a pendendo, item* Uirga, colis, *&c. Alia nomina solent imponi plurima, quae reticere praestat, quam nominare* (it is commonly called the penis, from pendulous, and also the rod, the stalk, etc. It is given many other names of which it is better to remain silent than to speak).[60] Although it was used by many writers of the sixteenth and seventeenth centuries with little sense of impropriety, the word penis itself was not always felt to be tonally neutral. In his *De dissectione partium corporis humani libri tres*, published in 1545, Charles Estienne quoted Cicero, *hodie [uerbum] penis est in obscoenis.*[61]

Bartholin reveals an odd mixture of prudery and delicacy in thinking about male sexuality when he turns from matters of diction

[59] Gabriello Falloppio, *Institutiones anatomicae* in *Opera genuina omnia* 3 vols (Venetiis 1606) I.10.
[60] Caspar Berthelsen Bartholin, *Institutiones anatomicae* (1611) new edn (Goslariae 1633) 119. See below for a discussion of words used in writing of the male sexual organs.
[61] Charles Estienne, *De dissectione partium corporis humani libri tres* (Parisiis 1545) 195. Cicero, *Ad familiares* 9.22.2. The whole of Cicero's letter concerns real or imagined obscenities.

to write about the size of the penis. He comments that it is variable but adds that in general the human penis is proportionately shorter than those of many lower animals. This is so, he alleges, because the human method of copulation, different from that of the brutes, does not need so long a penis:

> *In proportione uero breuior, quam in multis brutis, ob modum congressus in genere humano, qui non fit more brutorum.* (120)

He presumably has in mind the familiar "missionary position," repeatedly singled out by theologians of the middle ages and renaissance as the only acceptable method.[62] Bartholin must surely have known that, contrary to what he writes, copulation from the rear allows for deeper penetration. He nevertheless prefers to think of the human sexual anatomy as indicative of more restraint than is to be found among the lower animals.

It is common to find the more explicit commentators describing the erect penis as eight fingers in length.[63] An oddity, coupled with another farmyard comparison, is, however, found in Alexander Read's description of the vagina, which, in common with many others, he calls the neck of the uterus:

> In women of an ordinary stature, it is eight inches in length.
> The substance of this part is hard, without fleshy, within membranous and wrinckled, like to the inner skin of the upper jaw of a cowes mouth. (123)

---

[62] In addition to being a doctor, Caspar Berthelsen Bartholin was himself a theologian. For coital positions see James A. Brundage, "Let me count the ways: canonists and theologians contemplate coital positions," *Journal of medieval history* 10.2 (June 1984) 81-93 and Hart and Stevenson, *Heaven and the flesh* 31-38.

[63] Taken literally, this is equivalent (in the case of my fingers) to 16 cm—a perhaps satisfactory average figure.

In the next chapter he describes the uterus. Writing of its orifice (the cervix), and seeming not to have noticed how greatly he has exaggerated the length of the vagina, he says that "in the act of generation it may be so dilated that it will receive the glans of a mans genitall," thus implying that the length of an erect penis normally exceeds eight inches.

While the tone of Laurentius's initial linguistic discussion of the genitals is decidedly deadpan, he shows an unusual degree of interest in how to name the penis. Attributing the wealth of words to whoremongers, pimps, and vulgar girls, he lists eighteen Greek words, followed by fifteen in Latin, many of which have no simple equivalent in English: *penis, hasta, muto, uerpa, mentula, priapus, scapus, ueretrum, coles, caulis, uirga, fascinus uirilis, cauda salax, neruus fistularis, genitale* (approximately: tail, spear, penis, aroused penis, prick, phallus, shaft, shameful private parts, stem, stalk, rod, the male charm, the lascivious tail, the pipelike sinew, the [male] member).[64] Citing Laurentius in the opening paragraph of his chapter on the penis, Crooke affects modesty: "Many other names it hath both in Greek and Latine, a Catalogue whereof *Laurentius* hath put downe unnecessary for our turne, wherefore we have spared our owne labour and your eares" (210). Along with many other writers of his day Crooke commonly refers to the penis as "the yard," a synonym with little emotional colouring. While Crooke wished to avoid adding to the list of Greek and Latin names for the penis he might have been less troubled if he had confined himself to English. It is notable that although Latin *mentula* was considered a gross obscenity, the English language, at least in recent centuries, has reserved its strongest obscenities for references to women. "Prick," "tool," and "balls" appear to be heard as far less coarse than "cunt."

When Read translated the passage from Bartholin deriving penis from *a pendendo* he added a gloss: "It is called in Latin *Penis, a*

---

[64] Laurentius, *Anatomia humani corporis* 342. For the connotations of these and other terms, see the index to J. N. Adams, *The Latin sexual vocabulary* (London 1982).

pendendo, because it hangeth without the belly."[65] Recasting Read, Gibson follows that sentence with a further comment on names:

> Also *Uirga*, *Membrum uirile*, *Ueretrum*, *Mentula*, and by many other names invented by lustfull persons and lascivious Poets. (124)

A more common, simpler account such as Read's, little concerned with verbal distinctions, is succinct, plain, factual:

> it is an organicall part, long and round, yet somewhat flat in the upper part, seated about the lower part of the *os pubis*, appointed for making of water, and conveying the seed into the matrix. (113)

Some writers, among them Crooke (204), explain that the testes are so named because they are witnesses to virility. It is also common to find mention of the Greek word, δίδυμοι, twins. Graaf (4) adds further names: *poma amoris, bracchia mala, globuli naturales, colei* (the fruit of love, the evil [or ugly] limbs, the little globes of nature, the *colei* ["balls": a popular word for the testes, like French *couilles*, which is derived from it]). The most common word, used by doctors and writers generally with little affect, is "stones."[66]

The scrotum is named, sometimes with the explanation that it is the Latin word for a leather bag, which is the image that virtually all writers have in mind. Graaf (15) offers variants: *bursa uirilis* (the male purse), and *marsuppium* (a bag or pouch). *Scortum*, of which *scrotum* may be a variant, usually means leather or hide. A second meaning, which may add a degree of colouration, is a prostitute, including a male prostitute. Bartholin (137) also comments on the raphe under the scrotum, calling it a *sutura*, evoking the image of a stitched leather bag. The primary image is of a container designed to hold something precious and vulnerable, the delicacy of the testicles being frequently mentioned. Writing of the testicles Crooke adds:

---

[65] Read, *The manuall of the anatomy or dissection of the body of man* 113.
[66] See also above, 39n44.

"because it was neither profitable nor handsome that they should hang bare, for the receiving and cloathing of them, the *scrotum* or Cod was made as a purse or bagge" (204).

Nouns and verbs

The anatomists were mainly focused on taxonomy and discrimination. Nouns, with some adjectival coloration, were their primary linguistic territory. As objects for study and analysis, bodies needed to be both imagined as static and, in practice, seen as such in the dissection theatre. It seems both tendentious and teleological to attribute to this obvious way of advancing knowledge an ideological implication. One could not, in those years, study the muscles of an athlete when he was running, much less the function of the genitalia in sexual intercourse.[67] The movement of the planets was slow enough to make possible quasi static analysis of the universe illustrated by fixed diagrams. Static sexual structures needed to be examined before sexual functions could be understood. That the study of those structures with a nounal bias—taking little account of verbal function—should often have led anatomists astray is to be expected. A grasp of static pattern was the first goal, and progress from known patterns to the hitherto unknown is perhaps most readily achieved by the use of analogy. What, in the commonly observable physical world, do a woman's *labia minora* resemble? To mention the throat appendages of a cock is both moderately accurate and communicative. Similarly, anyone who has had his hand inside a cow's mouth will understand the analogy with the rugosity of the vagina. These are not, I believe, reductions of women to the status of farmyard animals; rather they are the readiest physical analogies which will convey something like the best understanding to the enquiring reader, just as the glans of the penis is so called because it looks more or less like an acorn. There is, too, the larger issue

---

[67] For such a study, see Willibrord Weijmar Schultz *et al.*, "Magnetic resonance imaging of male and female genitals during coitus and female sexual arousal," *British medical journal* 319 (18-25 December 1999) 1596-1600.

suggested by Crooke's having called his book a microcosmography. The term is familiar in the period; the idea of man as a microcosm, a little created world, had long been a cliché. The world was generally perceived as essentially an unchanging entity, subject to no more than local transformations until the second coming and the end of time. It is not surprising that the first anatomical enterprise should be to map part to part, using detailed knowledge of the fixed macrocosm to understand the equally fixed microcosm, as, in poetry, Phineas Fletcher was to do in *The purple island* (1633). In his long statement of the need to include a study of the genitals for the sake of completeness, Crooke had made the point slightly earlier than Fletcher: "The whole body is the Epitomie of the world, containing therein whatsoever is in the large universe" (197). His anatomical studies, a "Peregrination," involve him in constant movement: he explores, circles around the object of attention, pauses, says that he "entred into deliberation with" himself, considers whether, in relation to a study of the genitals, he "were best silently to passe it by." Carefully controlled by reason and design, the investigation is focused on something fixed. The end product of those studies, explorations, peregrinations is itself something fixed: not only is the human body a microcosm, but the resulting book is analogous to a body: without an examination of the genitals the book would be lame, would want a limb; with it the work will be completed, *consummatum*, "accomplished."

Crooke makes a plea for the preservation of the whole species by means of a study of the individual, again implying the primacy of taxonomic principles: "how much it is more expedient that the whole *kinde* should be preserved then any particular." The nounal emphasis is closely linked to the primacy of sight in these investigations: the close scrutiny of the cadaver on the dissecting table, the prurient desire of the elders to examine the details of the innocent Susannah's body, the delight which Gaveston's imagined audience hopes to experience when gazing at the chaste Diana. The evaluation of what was perceived was dependent on attitudes to the value of the world in its fallen state. Some, like Taliacotius, celebrated the enduring beauty of God's created beings; others were more inclined to see in fallen man's sexual equipment clear physical evidence of the misery and sinfulness of the modern world. Many patristics, including especially Augustine, had written of the innocence of prefallen sexual life; none, as far as I know, made explicit comments about appropriate responses to prefallen genitalia. While that is not, perhaps, surprising, it offers a contrast with the many remarks celebrating the divine nature of man: his upright stance, his tendency to gaze at the stars rather than at the ground, his godlike image.

Although Crooke says "containing therein whatsoever is in" rather than something like "functioning as does," some verbs do, of course, play a part in the descriptions. Crooke again implies an active rather than a passive approach to the body when he says "As for such as thinke there is no other principle of goodnesse then not to know evill, I would wish them to learne of their horses, that it is no good Mannage to stand stocke still but to move in order."[68] The frequent puzzled responses to the phrases *diductis labiis* and *citra sectionem*, with their implications of intervention—separating and (apparently) severing—reveal both fascination with and discomfort at imagining male interference with the vulva. In most cases, however, the use of verbs in conjunction with the activity of the vulva is focused more on ways in which female sexual organs inhibit or prevent function rather than actively promote it. Crooke's comments on the guiding, shielding functions of the labia are characteristic (237, see above). The structures of the genital organs, both male and female, are understood to be protective rather than aggressive, assertive. Verbal function is here designed to ensure stasis rather than development or exploration. The old obsession with virginity seems to be in play. A minor exception to the generally static image of the labia is found in Graaf, who also writes of their guiding function but in this case with reference to sexual activity: *Usus huius Rimae est canalis modo Penem tanquam in fossam dirigere* (the use of this cleft is so to speak to guide the penis, in the manner of a channel, into the ditch) (197).

Some tracts give advice about lovemaking. A long and explicit passage in Avicenna offers sound and simple advice about foreplay,

---

[68] See above, 10, 11.

comments occasionally repeated by later writers.[69] The *mons ueneris* was commonly understood to be a fleshy cushion serving to protect the groins of both partners. When writing of it Thomas Gibson uses metaphorical but active language. He calls it "the Hill of *Venus* which all those that will war in the Camp of *Venus* must first ascend" (157).[70] While much action is imagined, these passages, referring to the activity of the whole person, imply little about the activity of the sexual organs themselves, their responses and physical changes. Crooke, however, shows how these matters can be raised once the primary descriptive work has been completed. The individual books of his anatomy are in each case followed by a summary of controversial points. The *Controversies of the fourth booke* (241-56) is more focused than is book iv itself on verbs, on change, on function. Crooke attends to the process of erection of the penis, to the action of first penetrating a virgin, to the supposed motions of the womb and its sometimes violent reactions to smell and taste. While the male was conventionally understood to embody an active principle and the female a passive, so encouraging the static scrutiny of the female genitals, there was also a competing and troubling view of the vulva as voracious, apparently closed and quiet, but waiting, like a dozing monster, to guide the penis into its furrow and devour a man, and of the uterus as a roving beast largely out of control, ideas going at least as far back as to Plato (*Timaeus* 91a-d).[71] Although it was becoming obsolete by his time, Crooke reflects that old imagery.

That it should all have been fraught is not surprising. Crooke made a strong plea for the appropriateness of confronting and explaining the genitalia: "God that Created them, did he not intend their preservation, or can they bee preserved and not knowne? or knowne

---

[69] See above, 17n10, Avicenna. See also Magninus Mediolanensis, *Regimen sanitatis* (14C), II.vii and Paré, *The workes* 889-90, *Les oeuvres* 914-15.

[70] This metaphor, along with many other passages, is taken straight from Graaf, whom Gibson frequently acknowledges: *quem in Ueneris castris militaturi primum conscendere debent* (170).

[71] See, for example, Helen King, *Hippocrates' woman: reading the female body in ancient Greece* (London 1998) esp. 222-25.

and not discovered?" Others, however, looked forward to a time when men would no longer have to give thought to such matters. Juan Huarte had mentioned the angels, who do not have "the instruments . . . of generation" while in heaven men will be pleased to see their naked bodies since "the use of those parts, which were wont to offend the hearing and the eies, is now surceased" (267), a poor response, perhaps, to God's prefall command: Be fruitful, and multiply (Gen. 1.28).

APPENDIX

Midwifery

Guillaume de la Motte was troubled that before the end of the seventeenth century midwifery had been "in the hands of ignorant women."[72] Before the eighteenth century, when men began to dominate the profession, nearly all midwives were female, ranging from the tolerably well educated to the illiterate.[73] Those physicians and anatomists who wrote handbooks intended to assist them in their craft necessarily wrote simply and in the vernacular. The main aim was to give practical advice rather than to advance anatomical science. Percival Willughby (1596-1685), who was strongly critical of contemporary methods, is explicit:

> I have put forth these observations in English, knowing that few of our midwives bee learned in severall languages. For I have been with some that could not read, with severall that could not write; with many that understood very little of practice, and for such as these bee, it would do no good to

---

[72] Guillaume Mauquest de La Motte, *Traité complet des accouchemens naturels, non naturels et contre nature* (1715) trans. Thomas Tomkyns as *A general treatise of midwifry* (London 1746) iii.

[73] For the growing dominance of men in obstetric practice see Jean Donnison, *Midwives and medical men: a history of the struggle for control of childbirth* (1977) (London 1988).

speak to them of the anatomizing of the womb, or to tell them of . . . learned workes . . .[74]

The books are filled with case studies, descriptions of manipulative techniques, recipes for ointments, clysters, emetics, restorative drinks.[75] In many cases the appearance and general structure of the genitals are discussed only briefly if at all. In his preface La Motte excuses himself. The use here of the masculine pronoun may be no more than grammatical:

> Tho' anatomy has been always my chief delight, I touch upon it but very slightly in this treatise, taking it for granted, that my reader would not apply himself to the study of midwifry before he was sufficiently acquainted with the parts of generation.
>
> For the same reason I have omitted giving any plates of those parts, as they tend, by their loose representations to corrupt the manners of young people. They would, indeed, admit of some sort of excuse, if after the manner of the *Turks*, with whom the learned in the law are alone allowed to read their books, those I speak of were trusted into the hands of surgeons only. (viii)

There are notable exceptions. François Mauriceau's *The diseases of women with child* opens with "An anatomical treatise of the parts of a woman destin'd to generation." "I think it not amiss," he writes, "to premise, not only a Description of the Womb, but also of every

---

[74] Percival Willughby, *Observations in midwifery* (17th century, first edn 1863) ed. Henry Blenkinsop (Wakefield 1972) 2.

[75] Characteristic examples are Louise Bourgeois, *Observations diverses sur la sterilité, perte de fruict, foecondité, accouchement et maladies des femmes et enfants nouveaux nais* (1609) and Jacques Guillemeau, *De l'heureux accouchement des femmes* (1609) trans. as *Child-birth or, the happy deliverie of women* (London 1612). When commenting on Guillemeau and Mauriceau (see below) I focus on the translations which adopt and vary terms already established in the English tradition. Guillemeau's book went through many editions.

Part destin'd to Generation in a Woman: . . . 'tis impossible truly to apprehend what hereafter I pretend to teach, if these Parts be not perfectly understood." He will nevertheless be succinct: "I intend to be as brief upon them as I can, that Midwives may the easier reap the Benefit, (being unwilling to confound them with a multitude of Anatomical Controversies, for their sakes here omitted, as wholly unprofitable to them)."[76] He first offers two rather crude, oversimplified annotated figures in the general style of those found in the renaissance anatomy books. The annotations are standard: womb, lips, clitoris, *nymphae*, caruncles, vagina. Those to the third figure[77] include a description with two further terms for the cleft of he vulva: "The two great Lips of the Privy Parts, between which appears the great Crevice or Notch" (xxvi). Those to the fourth include a homely comparison, more emotionally charged, perhaps, than the descriptions of the *labia minora* as like a cock's wattles. Writing of the outward ends of the "testicles" (ovaries) he notes "The ragged piece, which is nothing but a Production or Extension of the broad Ligament, appearing ragged at the Ends, as if gnawn with Worms" (xxvii). Later, writing of the lower ligaments of the uterus, he says that they have the "Form of a Goose Foot" (xxxiii). More in keeping with classical imagery he calls the whole group of female genital organs a "fruitful Field" (xxvii-xxviii).[78]

Unexpectedly late in his opening treatise Mauriceau includes a brief paraphrase of what had by then become a standard description of the female genital organs (cf., above, *sine diductione/citra sectionem*):

> some . . . appear outwardly of their own accord, and the rest are concealed within these, and cannot be seen, unless the two great Lips are stretched asunder, and the Entry of the Privities a little opened. The Parts appearing need no description. The Parts hidden behind, or between these, are

---

[76] François Mauriceau, *Des maladies des femmes grosses et accouchées* (1668) trans. Hugh Chamberlen as *The diseases of women with child, and in child-bed* (1673) (London 1710) xvii.

[77] Lacking in this edition of the translation.

[78] Guillemeau writes of the "field of nature" (3).

the *Clitoris*, the Urinary Passage, the two *Nymphes*, and the four Caruncles. (xxxv)

He goes on to make further conventional remarks about the organs, naming the clitoris ("the *Woman's Yard*") and "the Navicular Ditch" (xxxv, xxxvi). He also repeats the misreading of Bartholin's comment that the caruncles do not wear away even in those who have frequently copulated and given birth.[79] He ends by saying "This almost is all can be said touching the privy Parts, and these others appertaining to them" (xxxvii). Although "touching" here means in the first place "concerning," the choice of word is suggestive.

Of greater interest than the well intentioned though often misguided manuals written by male anatomists and doctors are the midwifery books written by literate women. Of these the best known and most important is Jane Sharp's *The midwives book* (1671). In her introductory chapter she puts her faith in practice rather than in learned taxonomy:

It is not hard words that perform the work, as if none understood the Art that cannot understand Greek. Words are but the shell, that we ofttimes break our Teeth with them to come at the kernel, I mean our brains to know what is the meaning of them; but to have the same in our mother tongue would save us a great deal of needless labour. (3-4)

The first section (book i) is devoted to "A brief description of the Generative parts in both sexes." Compared to many others, her description, filling seventyfive pages (5-80), is not at all brief. The style is loose, with many repetitions and contradictions. She quotes and paraphrases passages from some of the more familiar anatomical treatises of earlier decades, placing special reliance on Crooke and on Culpeper's *A directory for midwives* (1651, 1656). She also repeats popular lore such as that boys are bred in the right side of the womb, girls in the left (38), and the outdated idea that women's genitalia are inversions of those of men (37, 40-41; but with strong

---

[79] See above, 36-37.

qualifications on 82). Although no original thinker, she demonstrates forthright common sense: "Man can do nothing without the woman to beget Children, though some idle Coxcombs will needs undertake to shew how Children may be had without use of the woman" (41); her tone is tart as she comments: "They that maintain . . . a woman can have but two Children at once because nature hath given her but two breasts, she may as well go but two Miles because she hath but two legs" (69).

Clearing the way for her necessary focus on the female organs, Jane Sharp first describes the male genitals. While she makes a conventional plea for appropriate responses, there is no hint of the painful embarrassment which overwhelmed so many of her male contemporaries and forebears:

> because it is commonly maintain'd, that the Masculine gender is more worthy than the Feminine, though perhaps when men have need of us they will yield the priority to us; that I may not forsake the ordinary method, I shall begin with men, and treat last of my own sex, so as to be understood by the meanest capacity, desiring the Courteous Reader to use as much modesty in the perusal of it, as I have endeavoured to do in the writing of it, considering that such an Art as this cannot be set forth, but that young men and maids will have much just cause to blush sometimes, and be ashamed of their own follies, as I wish they may if they shall chance to read it, that they may not convert that into evil that is really intended for a general good. (4-5)

She uses homely words: the raphe under the scrotum she calls a seam (10), the glans is the "Head or Nut of the Yard" which is "made like to a top, that it may enter the better" (19, 27); the urethra is a "great pipe" (25); of the testicles she writes "some call them Eggs" (10). Writing of the muscles of the penis, which were thought to be the primary cause of erection, she says "besides that they raise the Yard to make it stand, they also bend the fore part of the Yard to be thrust into the womb, so that all things are so exactly fitted by nature, that a blind man cannot miss it" (29). She offers her own version of the many statements that the location of the penis is familiar to everyone: "It stands in the sharebone in the middle as all know" (19, cf. above, 28n23). Towards the end of her discussion of the male genitals she repeats and develops an earlier comment she had made about circumcision (21). Reporting that some thought copulation "migh [*sic*] be better performed" without the foreskin, she writes:

> the *Jews* indeed were commanded to be Circumcised, but now Circumcision avails not & is forbidden by the Apostle. I hope no man will be so void of reason and Religion, as to be Circumcised to make trial which of these two opinions is the best; but the world was never without some mad men, who will do any thing to be singular: were the foreskin any hindrance to procreation or pleasure, nature had never made it, who made all things for these very ends and purposes. (31-32)

Her account of the female genitals is, as one might expect, focused mainly on impregnation and the function of the uterus. In passing she nevertheless includes more frequent comment than is usual with her male counterparts on the pleasures of copulation. Writing of the width of the vagina she reports a lament sometimes still heard in modern times:

> I have heard a *French* man complain sadly, that when he first married his Wife, it was no bigger nor wider than would fit his turn, but now it was grown as a Sack; Perhaps the fault was not the womans but his own, his weapon shrunk and was grown too little for the scabbard" (53).

While her words for the genital organs are in most cases standard, she offers some simple synonyms. The "great cleft" she calls a cut (20, 37) and a slit (43); the womb, as in Guillemeau, is the "Field of Nature" (63; cf. Mauriceau's "fruitful Field"). The problematical four caruncles she describes as "like a Rose half blown when the bearded leaves are taken away, or this production with the Lap or privity is like a great Clove-gilleflower new blown, thence came the word deflowred" (48). Describing the mouth of the womb—the cervix—she repeats Columbus' remark that it resembles "the head of a Tench," but in place of his *uel canini oris* she writes "or of a young Kitten" (35).[80]

At the end of book i, she again reassures her readers that she has tried to use only plain language. Perhaps echoing the desire of the Royal Society for simplicity and clarity, she is concerned to give practical advice rather than to indulge in logic chopping or etymological speculation:

> Thus I have as briefly and as plainly as I could, laid down a description of the parts of generation of both sexes, purposely omitting hard names, that I might have no cause to enlarge my work, by giving you the meaning of them where there is no need, unless it be for such persons who desire rather to know Words than Things. (80)

---

[80] In common with others, she confuses *perineum* and *peritoneum* (38). See above, 15n8. Further notes on Jane Sharp's sources and style are found in Elaine Hobby's excellent modern edition (New York and London 1999).

Bibliography

Adams, J. N. *The Latin sexual vocabulary* (London 1982).

Alemán, Mateo. *Guzmán de Alfarache* (1599, 1604) trans. James Mabbe as *The rogue* (London 1623).

Almond, Philip C. *Heaven and hell in enlightenment England* (Cambridge 1994).

Anon. *An other defence of womens vertues, written by an honorable personage of great reckoning in Fraunce*, appended to *A womans woorth, defended against all the men in the world. Prooving them to be more perfect, excellent and absolute in all vertuous actions, then any man of what qualitie soever*, a translation, perhaps by Anthony Munday, of Alexandre de Pont-Aymeri's *Paradoxe apologique, ou il est fidellement démonstré que la femme est beaucoup plus parfaite que l'homme en toute action de vertu* (Paris 1594) (London 1599).

Anon. *Aristotle's masterpiece* (1684) (London 1704).

Avicenna. *Liber canonis* (11th century) trans. Gerard of Cremona (Basileae 1556).

Banister, John. *The historie of man* (London 1578).

Bartholin, Caspar Berthelsen. *Institutiones anatomicae* (1611) new edn (Goslariae 1632).

Bartholin, Thomas. *Anatomia, ex Caspari Bartholini parentis institutionibus . . . reformata* (Hagae-Comitis 1655).

——. *Bartholinus anatomy; made from the precepts of his father* . . . published by Nicholas Culpeper and Abdiah Cole (London 1663).

Bauhin, Kaspar. *Institutiones anatomicae corporis virilis et muliebris* (1597) (Geneva? 1604).

——. *Theatrum anatomicum* (Francofurti 1605).

Blanckaert, Steven (Stephen Blancard). *A physical dictionary: in which, all the terms relating either to anatomy, chirurgery, pharmacy, or chymistry, are very accurately explain'd* trans. J. G. (1684) 2nd edn, enlarged (London 1693).

Bonaciolus, Ludovicus. *Muliebrium libri II* (late 15th century) in Caspar Wolf (ed.) *Gynaeciorum . . . libri veterum ac recentiorum* (Basileae 1566) cols 553-770.

Bourgeois, Louise. *Observations diverses sur la sterilité, perte de fruict, foecondité, accouchement et maladies des femmes et enfants nouveaux nais* (Paris 1609).

Brundage, James A. "Let me count the ways: canonists and theologians contemplate coital positions," *Journal of medieval history* 10.2 (June 1984) 81-93.

Cadden, Joan. *Meanings of sex difference in the middle ages: medicine, science, and culture* (Cambridge 1993).

Chernaik, Warren. *Sexual freedom in restoration literature* (Cambridge 1995).

Cohen, Rev. Dr A. *Proverbs: Hebrew text and English translation with an introduction and commentary* (Hindhead 1945).

Columbus, Realdus. *De re anatomica libri xv* (Venetiis 1559).

Constantinus Africanus. *De coitu* in *Opera* (Basileae 1536) 299-307.

Crooke, Helkiah. *Μικροκοσμογραφία. A description of the body of man* (1615) 2nd edition, enlarged (London 1631).

Culpeper, Nicholas. *A directory for midwives* (London 1651).

Dalton, Michael. *The countrey justice, conteyning the practise of the justices of the peace out of their sessions* (London 1618).

Donnison, Jean. *Midwives and medical men: a history of the struggle for control of childbirth* (1977) (London 1988).

Duden, Barbara. *The woman beneath the skin: a doctor's patients in eighteenth-century Germany* (1987) trans. Thomas Dunlap (Cambridge, Mass., 1991).

Estienne, Charles. *De dissectione partium corporis humani libri tres* (Parisiis 1545).

Ettmüller, Michael. *Opera omnia* (Lugduni 1685).

Falloppio, Gabriello. *Institutiones anatomicae* in *Opera genuina omnia* 3 vols (Venetiis 1606) I.1-36.

Galen. *On the usefulness of the parts of the body* trans. Margaret Tallmadge May 2 vols (Ithaca, NY, 1968).

Gibson, Thomas. *The anatomy of humane bodies epitomized* (London 1682).

Graaf, Regnerus de. *De mulieribus organis generationi inservientibus* in *Opera omnia* (Lugduni Batavorum 1677).

Guillemeau, Jacques. *De l'heureux accouchement des femmes* (1609) trans. as *Child-birth, or the happy deliverie of women* (London 1612).

Hart, Clive and Kay Gilliland Stevenson. *Heaven and the flesh* (Cambridge 1995).

Huarte, Juan. *Examen de ingenios* (1575), trans. (into Italian) by Camillo Camilli and (thence into English) by Richard Carew as *The examination of mens wits* (London 1594).

James, Robert. *A medicinal dictionary* 3 vols (London 1743, 1745).

Keynes, Geoffrey. *The life of William Harvey* (Oxford 1966).

King, Helen. *Hippocrates' woman: reading the female body in ancient Greece* (London 1998).

La Motte, Guillaume Mauquest de. *Traité complet des accouchemens naturels, non naturels et contre nature* (1715) trans. Thomas Tomkyns as *A general treatise of midwifry* (London 1746).

Laurentius, Andreas (= André du Laurens, *d.* 1609). *Anatomia humani corporis* (Parisiis 1600).

Magninus Mediolanensis. *Regimen sanitatis* (14C) (Louaniensi 1482). A variation of a work by Arnaldus de Villa Nova (d. 1313?)

Mandeville, Bernard. *Wishes to a godson, with other miscellany poems* (London 1712).

Marlowe, Christopher. *The tragedy of Edward II* (1594) in *The works of Christopher Marlowe* ed. C. F. Tucker Brooke (Oxford 1910).

Marten, John. *Gonosologium novum: or, a new system of all the secret infirmities and diseases, natural, accidental, and venereal in men and women* (London 1709). Appended to the sixth edition of his *A treatise of all the degrees and symptoms of the venereal disease in both sexes* (London 1708?).

Maupertuis, Pierre-Louis Moreau de. *Vénus physique* (1745) in *Oeuvres* II new edn (Lyon 1756) 1-133.

Mauriceau, François. *Les maladies des femmes grosses et accouchées* (1668) trans. Hugh Chamberlen as *The diseases of women with child, and in child-bed* (1673) (London 1710).

O'Malley, C. D. "Helkiah Crooke, M. D., F. R. C. P., 1576-1648," *Bulletin of the history of medicine* 42.1 (January-February 1968) 1-18.

Paré, Ambroise. *Les oeuvres* (1575) 8th edition (Paris 1628). Trans. Thomas Johnson as *The workes* (London 1634).

Park, Katharine. "The rediscovery of the clitoris: French medicine and the tribade, 1570-1620" in David Hillman and Carla Mazzio, edd, *The body in parts: fantasies of corporeality in early modern Europe* (New York and London 1997) 171-93.

Pineau, Séverin. *De virginitatis notis, graviditate & partu* (1597) (Lugduni Batavorum 1650).

Porter, Dorothy and Roy Porter. *Doctors and doctoring in eighteenth-century England* (Cambridge 1989).

Porter, Roy and Mikuláš Teich, edd. *Sexual knowledge, sexual science: the history of attitudes to sexuality* (Cambridge 1994).

Quincy, John, M. D. *Lexicon physico-medicum: or, a new physical dictionary* (London 1719).

Raynalde, Thomas. *The birth of mankind* (1545) "4th edn" (London 1654). An augmented version of Richard Jonas's translation of Roesslin (see below).

Read, Alexander. *The manuall of the anatomy or dissection of the body of man* (London 1612).

——. Σωματογραφία ανθροπίνε, *or a description of the body of man* (1616) (London 1634). A compendium from Crooke.

——. *A treatise of all the muscles of the body of man* (London 1659) in *The workes* 3rd edn (London 1659).

Roesslin, Eucharius. *Der swangern Frawen und Hebammen Rosegarten* (Strasburg 1512?)

Rufus of Ephesus (1st-2nd centuries AD). [On the names of the parts of the human body] in *Oeuvres* ed. Charles Daremberg and Charles Émile Ruelle (1879) (Amsterdam 1963) 133-67. Greek text with French translation.

Sawday, Jonathan. *The body emblazoned* (London and New York 1995).

Sharp, Jane. *The midwives book, or the whole art of midwifry discovered, directing childbearing women how to behave themselves* (London 1671). Modern edition by Elaine Hobby (New York and Oxford 1999).

Spach, Israel (ed.). *Gynaeciorum sive de mulierum affectibus commentarii* 3 vols (Basileae 1586). An expanded version of Wolf (below).

Speert, Harold. *Obstetric and gynecologic milestones* (1958) (New York 1996).

——. *Obstetrics and gynecology: a history and iconography* (San Francisco 1994).

Stockhamer, Franciscus. Μικροκοσμογραφία, *sive partium humani corporis omnium earumque actionem & usuum brevis quidem, accurata tamen & atoma descriptio novis hujus saeculi inventis exornata* (Viennae Austriae 1682).

Swammerdam, Johannes. *Miraculum naturae sive uteri muliebris fabrica notis in D. Joh. van Horne prodromum illustrata, & tabulis* (Lugduni Batavorum 1672).

Taliacotius, Gaspar (Gaspare Tagliacozzi, 1545-99). *De curtorum chirurgia per insitionem* (Venetiis 1597).

Verheyen, Philip. *Corporis humani anatomiae liber primus . . . secundus* 2nd edition (Bruxellis 1710).

Vesalius, Andreas. *De humani corporis fabrica* (Basileae 1543).

Wagner, Peter. *Eros revived: erotica of the enlightenment in England and America* (London 1988).

Weijmar Schultz, Willibrord, *et al.*, "Magnetic resonance imaging of male and female genitals during coitus and female sexual arousal," *British medical journal* 319 (18-25 December 1999) 1596-1600.

Willughby, Percival. *Observations in midwifery* (17th century, first edn 1863) ed. Henry Blenkinsop (Wakefield 1972).

Wolf, Caspar (ed.). *Gynaeciorum . . . libri veterum ac recentiorum* (Basileae 1566).

Index